The Ten Granted Paradise

DR. SAYED AMMAR NAKSHAWANI

ACKNOWLEDGEMENTS

I would like to thank Nebil Husayn for his valuable and insightful comments leading to a wonderful and important introduction. I would also like to thank Zain Moloobhoy, Nicole Correri and Zehra Jafri for their kind editing of this work. I give my thanks to Team SAN for their unwavering support in all projects.

I am grateful for the support of UMAA and The Abidi Foundation and give my thanks to both.

- Dr. Sayed Ammar Nakshawani

DEDICATION

I dedicate this book to my beloved dear friends, two flowers from heaven, Yousef Zayni and Ahmed Kadum Ali al-Kurbasi (Abu Ali).

Table of Contents

BLESSING UPON THE ATTESTERS TO THE MESSENGERS

O Allah, as for the followers of the messengers and those of the people of the earth who attested to them unseen (while the obstinate resisted them through crying lies) - they yearned for the emissaries through the realities of faith, in every era and time in which Thou didst send a messenger and set up for the people a director from the period of Adam down to Muhammad (Blessings of Allah upon Him and His Household) from among the Imams of guidance and the leaders of the godfearing (upon them all be peace) - remember them with forgiveness and good pleasure!

O Allah, and as for the Companions of Muhammad specifically, those who did well in companionship, who stood the good test in helping him, responded to him when he made them hear his messages' argument, separated from mates and children in manifesting his word, fought against fathers and sons in strengthening his prophecy, and through him gained victory; those who were wrapped in affection for him, hoping for a commerce that comes not to naught in love for him; those who were left by their clans when they clung to his handhold and denied by their kinsfolk when they rested in the shadow of his kinship; forget not,

O Allah, what they abandoned for Thee and in Thee, and make them pleased with Thy good pleasure for the sake of the creatures they drove to Thee while they were with Thy Messenger, summoners to Thee for Thee. Show gratitude to them for leaving the abodes of their people for Thy sake and going out from a plentiful livelihood to a narrow one, and [show gratitude to] those of them who became objects of wrongdoing and whom Thou multiplied in exalting Thy religion.

O Allah, and give to those who have done well in following the Companions, who say, Our Lord, forgive us and our brothers who went before us in faith, Thy best reward; those who went straight to the Companions' road, sought out their course, and proceeded in their manner. No doubt concerning their sure insight diverted them and no uncertainty shook them from following in their tracks and being led by the guidance of their light. As their assistants and supporters, they professed their religion, gained guidance through their guidance, came to agreement with them, and never accused them in what they passed on to them.

O Allah, and bless the Followers, from this day of ours to the Day of Doom, their wives, their offspring, and those among them who obey Thee, with a blessing through which Thou wilt preserve them from disobeying Thee, make room for them in the plots of Thy Garden, defend them from the trickery of Satan, help them in the piety in which they seek help from Thee, protect them from sudden events that come by night and day - except the events which come with good - and incite them to tie firmly the knot of good hope in Thee, what is with Thee, and refrain from ill thoughts [toward Thee] because of what the hands of Thy servants' hold.

Thus Thou mayest restore them to beseeching Thee and fearing Thee, induce them to renounce the plenty of the immediate, make them love to work for the sake of the deferred and prepare for what comes after death, make easy for them every distress that comes to them on the day when souls take leave from bodies, release them from that which brings about the perils of temptation and being thrown down in the Fire and staying forever within it, and take them to security, the resting place of the godfearing.

- Imam Ali ibn Husayn, Zain ul Abideen (AS)

Al-Sahifa al-Sajjadiyya

Introduction

The Veneration of Companions in Imāmī Shī'ism

There are a number of noble figures venerated in the collective Muslim memory of Islamic history. The term "collective" signifies that memory which all Muslims who faced the Ka'ba at the end of the first century agreed upon. Whether they lived in Damascus and supported the Umayyads, in Kufa where many held Ali b. Abi Talib and his family in high esteem, or the Hijaz where many Muslims considered themselves the partisans of the first three caliphs and their descendants, each party possessed a memory of the past which praised their heroes and their wisdom. For example, in the Hijaz, the hadith and legal practice of Aisha bint Abi Bakr, the intellectual and spiritual inheritor of the first caliph, and 'Abd Allah ibn 'Umar, the inheritor of the second caliph, played an extremely important role in subsequent Sunni and Maliki teachings (ibn 'Umar especially in the latter case). In each of these political circles, a few Companions and their students became the subject of hadith and legendary tales about their merit, some of which later scholars of hadith concluded to be fabrications. In some cases, it is difficult to judge the authenticity of such reports, so an historian is left to provide a narrative that either acknowledges their existence or suppresses them.

A number of scholars (Shī'ī, Sunni and non-Muslim) claiming the authority to speak on behalf of the Shī'ī community have inappropriately characterized the sect as one that generally despises Companions of the Prophet, curses them, and considers them to have become apostates after his death (see ibn Taymiyya, E. Kohlberg). These misconceptions and hasty generalizations are not only derived from a cursory reading of a few Shī'ī texts and unrepresentative thinkers, but the second-hand authority of many writers with a clearly uninformed or anti-Shī'ī worldview. Such writers have opted to suppress or willfully ignore early, medieval, and modern Shī'ī authors who have cited various Shī'ī texts and the collective Sunnī-Shī'ī memory of the past that have praised a number of Companions (see Tusi, Amin, Musawi). Likewise, they have ignored Shī'ī commentaries and nuanced discussions regarding early Shī'ī hadith that appear "anti-Companion."

The Sunni historical tradition certainly recognized that days after the death of the Prophet and during the caliphates of Uthman, Ali, Hasan, and Yazid, the Muslim community was embroiled in conflict. The partisans of each group condemned the other, so it is no surprise that the Shī'ī intellectual history has preserved much of the criticism leveled against Ali's rivals. Sunni hadith and biographical literature likewise preserves the various ways in which partisans of Ali's rivals would condemn and curse him and his family. For example, Bukhari and other hadith specialists relied upon Harīz b. Uthman (d. 163

AH), a narrator who despised Ali for killing his ancestors at Siffin and claimed that Ali once tried to injure or kill the Prophet (see ibn Hajar, 2:210). Harīz would verbally abuse (*yasubb*) and pray for the damnation (*yal'an*) of Ali b. Abi Talib (see ibn Asakir, 12:348). Syrian soldiers fighting Ali at Siffin allegedly believed that he was a person who did not pray (see Tabari, 4:30). A canonical Sunni hadith likewise portrays Ali as disappointing the Prophet by refusing his invitation to join him in prayer (see Bukhari, 2:43, 8:155, 190; Muslim, 2:187, ibn Hanbal, 1:77, 91, 112).

Sunni orthodoxy eventually began to abstain from discussions about conflicts during those volatile periods so that the honour of any Muslim who met the Prophet remained intact. However, Shī'ism has continued to remain invested in analysing those conflicts, with the Household of the Prophet and those who sided with them portrayed as righteous, wise, and patient, while their rivals consistently appeared mistaken, confused, or regretful for opposing the Prophet's family.

Whether one sympathizes or disagrees with the views and conduct of Ali b. Abi Talib and his party, a researcher of Islamic history should consult a few studies (e.g. the works of W. Madelung and S.H.M Jafri) to become acquainted with the numerous Companions of the Prophet venerated in the Shī'ī and early pro-'Alid (or pro ahl al-bayt) Sunni tradition. One will conclude Shī'ī

antipathy for Ali's rivals may be true, but animosity toward
Companions as an entire group would be inaccurate.

Ironically, some Companions praised in the Shī'ī tradition are
attacked and/or ignored in the Sunni tradition, which claims to
venerate "all" Companions. Examples of Companions who are
attacked or whose pro-'Alid tendencies are considered problematic in
the Sunni tradition include Muhammad b. Abi Bakr, Hukaym b.
Jabala, Hujr b. Adi, Sulayman b. Surad al-Khuza'i, Muslim b.
'Awsaja and Abu Tufayl 'Amr b. Wathila. How does Sunnism view
the political careers and the trustworthiness of these pro-'Alid
Companions? Most Sunni thinkers will find the question unsettling
due to (1) an aversion to discussing events regarding the period
known as "fitna" and (2) the conduct of these Companions, which
seem to validate Shī'ī views regarding history.

Sayed Ammar Nakshawani in the following work not only
corrects the widespread misconception that the Shī'ī intellectual
tradition despises and curses all Companions, but also clarifies the
reason for which some Companions were considered people of
Paradise in the Shī'ī (and usually the Sunni) tradition. In a few
places, the author notes reasons for which the Imāmī tradition does
not venerate certain Companions. Many Muslims will likely find
those sections of the book controversial and contest the authenticity
of some of the relied upon reports. Discussing controversial history

as it relates to Companions and the ahl al-bayt remains a difficult enterprise, where methods and premises, let alone conclusions, substantially differ from scholar to scholar. What qualifies as "offensive"? Have Muslims developed a method to critically and fairly discuss issues that one party may consider offensive? Can such discussions occur without falling into polemics, where one assumes *a priori* the malicious intent of the opposition or the infallibility of one's own interpretation? The popularity of literalism and absolutism in many Muslim communities leaves prospects for any immediate change in the discourse bleak.

It is no secret that Sunnism, based on a famous hadith, generally presents a different list of "ten promised Paradise" consisting of revered political figures. For the benefit of the reader, critiques regarding the authenticity of the Sunni report within Shī'ism are cited below.

Sunni hadith literature famously names a list of "ten promised Paradise," beginning with the first four caliphs, Talhah, Zubayr, Sa'd b. Abi Waqqas, 'Abd al-Rahman b. 'Awf, Abu 'Ubaydah al-Jarrah and Sa'id b. Zayd. However, the report is doubted in the Imami tradition for a few reasons. First, the hadith is considered a "solitary report," which some theologians did not consider to be valid in establishing theological tenets. Second, the only Companion who may have narrated this report was Sa'id b. Zayd who included himself in the list. In light of the Qur'anic prohibition, "And do not claim purity for yourselves" (Q53:32), Shaykh al-Mufid argues that testimony attesting to one's own character is not considered authoritative in legal disputes (see *al-Ifsah*, p.71-89). The hadith of Sa'id can be rejected since other trustworthy witnesses besides the claimant himself have not corroborated it. Al-Mufid also cites one narrative in which Imam Ali heard the hadith, rejected its attribution to the Prophet, and considered it the claim of Sa'id (*al-Kafi' ah*, p. 24-5). According to al-Amīnī, recensions of the hadith that are attributed to 'Abd al-Rahman b. 'Awf (d. 32 AH) are unacceptable since there is a missing link between him and the next narrator, Hamīd b. 'Abd al-Rahman (d. 107 AH). Hamīd was either born a year after ibn 'Awf's death or in the same year (see *al-Ghadīr*, 10:122). Third, the hadith names the most famous political rivals of Ali and polemically guarantees their salvation, when members of the community hotly debated the righteousness and openly condemned some of these Companions for over a century (e.g. Talhah, Zubayr and Ali himself). Thus, the hadith reflects late second-century Sunni attempts to become non-partisan by rehabilitating all Companions as righteous rather than acknowledging earlier debates and tensions. Sunnism eventually claimed that all six individuals named in the council to elect the third caliph represented those surviving Companions promised Paradise. An indication of the non-existence of the hadith and/or this theological belief at the time of the election is Sa'id b. Zayd's conspicuous absence. Why doesn't 'Umar or anyone on the council request Sa'id's presence if the Prophet had named them all together? Finally, the hadith clearly ignores the names of (1) famous Ansar from Medina, (2) those Meccans guaranteed Paradise who were not from Quraysh (e.g. Ammar b. Yasir and his family), and (3) those who supported Ali's wars during his caliphate. The author includes members from these three excluded groups in the entries below.

As an expert of the Shī'ī tradition, Sayed Ammar Nakshawani presents relevant Shī'ī hagiographical narratives for non-specialists who would otherwise be unaware of them. Future historiographical studies can no longer ignore Imami literature that venerates Companions. Thus, the following biographies fill a lacuna in knowledge about Companions not only revered in the Shī'ī tradition, but according to the collective memory of pro-Alid Sunni and Shī'ī authors, granted Paradise.

Nebil Husayn
Princeton University

Works Cited

al-Amīn, Muḥsin. A'yān Al-Shī'ah. (Beirut: 1983).

al-Amīnī, 'Abd al-Ḥusayn. al-Ghadīr. (Beirut: 1977).

Bukhārī, Muḥammad b. Ismā'īl. Ṣaḥīḥ Al-Bukhārī. (Beirut: 1981)

Ibn 'Asākir, Hibat Allah. Tarīkh Madīna Dimashq. (Beirut: 1995).

Ibn Ḥajar, Aḥmad ibn Ḥajar al-'Asqalānī. Tahdhīb al-Tahdhīb. (Beirut: 1982).

Ibn Ḥanbal, Aḥmad. *Al-Musnad.* (Beirut: 1969).

Ibn Taymiyya, Aḥmad. *Majmū' Fatāwā Shaykh Al-Islām Aḥmad Ibn Taymiyya.* (Medina: 1995), vol. 28, p. 477.

Jafri, S.H.M. *The Origins and Early Development of Shi'a Islam.* (Oxford: 2003).

Kohlberg, Etan. 'Some Imami Shi'ī views of the Sahaba" *Jerusalem Studies in Arabic and Islam 5* 1984, p. 143-75.

Madelung, Wilferd. *Succession to Muhammad.* (Cambridge: 1996).

al-Mufīd, Muḥammad. *al-Iṣāḥ.* (Beirut: 1993).

--. *al-Kāfi'ah.* (Beirut: 1993).

al-Mūsawī, Sharaf al-Dīn. *al-Fuṣūl al-Muhimma,* (Tehran; n.d.), p. 189-200.

al-Qushayrī, Muslim ibn al-Ḥajjāj. *Al-Jāmi' al-Ṣaḥīh.* (Beirut: 1974).

al-Ṭabarī, Muḥammad b. Jarīr. *Ta'rīkh.* (Beirut: 1983).

al-Ṭūsī, Muḥammad. *Ikhtiyār ma'rifat al-rijāl.* (Qum: 1983).

Chapter 1

Salman al-Muhammadi

I am Salman, the son of Islam from the children of Adam

S alman al-Muhammadi occupies a prominent position in the religion of Islam and is regarded as one of the most loyal companions of the Holy Prophet (pbuh) and of Imam Ali (as). He is a personality who is revered in a number of different schools within the religion of Islam. Many of the Sufi sects trace much of their teachings back to Salman and he is also prominent within Alawi-Nusayri narratives. In the latter tradition, Salman is considered part of an esoteric three or a trinity consisting of Muhammad, Ali, and Salman. He is revered in every school within the religion of Islam and occupies an exalted position as an honorary member of the Ahl al-Bayt (as). In many narratives he is praised highly and portrayed as one who followed and protected the principles and the teachings of the family of the Holy Prophet (pbuh).

Every human being has the pursuit of happiness as a goal in his or her life in one way or another. However, Salman's life was a dedicated journey in pursuit of truth and thereby happiness. Salman faced many major struggles and hardships to achieve his goal. He faced struggles in terms of wealth, health, education, and family.

Salman represents the experience of converts to the religion of Islam as well. While all first Muslims were converts who faced tremendous pressures, losses, and difficulties to gain their Muslim identities, Salman is a particularly relevant role model.

The way he identified himself is how most converts see themselves today, as Muslims first and foremost. He moved from one religion to another and travelled over long distances seeking the truth. That migration from one land to another and one religion to another required a great amount of sacrifice, loss of family, friends, and connections. Salman lost all of these, but found the religion of Islam; indeed he found his true identity.

One day, a prominent Companion was sitting amongst a group in the Prophet's (pbuh) mosque waiting for the *adhan* to be called. In the presence of Umar ibn Khattab, this prominent Companion began to boast that he was from a certain tribe and requested others in the mosque to mention the identity of their tribes. Each one began to name his tribal heritage and the Quraysh were represented, as well as the Aws, Tamim, and so forth.

Salman was asked which tribe he was from and he replied, "I am the son of the religion of Islam. I was lost and I found guidance through Muhammad (pbuh). I was poor and I became rich through Muhammad (pbuh). I was a slave and I became free through Muhammad (pbuh)." Salman happily declared that Islam was his tribe and his primary identity. He, unlike the others, internalised the essence of Islam: the path to developing a true and accurate identity that would lead to more humane and ethical behaviour.

From the outset, Salman embodied this message of the Muslim identity. In today's mosques, when converts enter they are seen as outsiders instead of members of the family of Islam. The greatest welcome and sympathy should be extended towards them for the sacrifices they have gone through for this pursuit of truth.

Those born into the religion today see Islam as their own tribe and no one else's. Furthermore, each cultural group feels they are the ultimate devotees to the Ahl al-Bayt (as). This is a false pride on many levels, because Islam is an active religion, rather than a cultural identity one simply obtains as a birthright. Salman also exemplified the pursuit of truth in spite of time, distance, and difficulty, which remains at the heart of the religion.

Mutahhari expounds beautifully and quite emphatically on these factors that are central to an Islamic identity in his work, "The World View of Tawhid":

> Islam rejects and condemns every kind of obduracy
> [inflexible severity], obstinacy, fanaticism, blind
> imitativeness, partisanship, and selfishness, which are
> contrary to the spirit that seeks to realise truth and
> reality…blind imitation of parents, and submission to
> inherited traditions are condemned as contrary to the
> Islamic spirit of surrender…[which leads] to error,
> deviation, and remoteness from the truth. (76-77)

According to many reports, Salman was a couple of years older than the Holy Prophet (pbuh). His name was originally Ruzbeh and he was from a Persian family that practiced the religion of Zoroastrianism. Originally, this faith was similar to other monotheistic faiths, but with time developed into a dualist tradition. Salman's father was originally a land-owner and chief in a village located in modern-day Isfahan. His land ownings were vast and he used to own a great number of horses. Salman was born into a wealthy family and lived a prosperous lifestyle with many servants.

This comfortable life would be satisfying to many individuals. Although Salman was brought up in the lap of luxury, he still had the desire for greater meaning. His father noticed that from a young age, Salman was inquisitive about this world. Muhammad Jawad al-Faqih, in his series of books about the four Companions: Miqdad, Abu Dhar, Salman and Ammar, describes Salman as a monotheistic thinker and believer even as a young man.

Salman's father also noticed that he was very bright, but his father was very protective of his son and rarely let him out of his sight. At the age of sixteen, his father allowed him to be in charge of the temple of the Zoroastrians, which was seen as an honour. His duty would be to tend to the ever-burning flame in the temple. Salman took it upon himself to not only guard the flame at the temple, but also study Zoroastrian sacred texts and theology in order to learn more about the faith.

For three years, Salman read, studied, and even debated the high priest of the Zoroastrian faith. By the age of nineteen, he thought to himself that his questions were not being answered satisfactorily; he knew he had to continue his search. He desired to be guided to the truth and become enlightened.

One day, his father had some clients who had come to see some of his properties. He needed Salman to complete a task at his other estate that he could not do himself. Salman complied and went off to the property that was out of his usual way. On the way to the estate, he saw a building he had never seen before and heard beautiful voices echoing from within. His curiosity was piqued and he wanted to discover this place that was so different from his temple.

When he entered, he saw a group of men praying and he sat with them. He inquired about their beliefs, and they replied that they believed in God, the Prophets of old, Jesus Christ, and their holy book, the Bible, that speaks of a Day of Judgment. Salman immediately felt drawn to this group. He felt that he had now found the answer to his yearnings. He wanted to join their faith and they initiated him, but they told him that there were going to be a few obstacles for him.

Because his father was a renowned figure in the Zoroastrian religion, he would surely be displeased with his son's actions. The narrations state that Salman came home late that night and his father inquired as to where he had been and what he had been doing. Salman told him that he met a group of people with the most beautiful place of worship, where they lifted their voices in praise of God beseeching God's blessings.

They called themselves Christians and Salman described how their beliefs made sense to him. His father wouldn't hear of it; he would not allow him to join any other faith. His father decided that if he couldn't talk Salman out of it, then he would convince him by force. He barred Salman into his home, made him a prisoner, and even began torturing him, thinking that torture would force Salman to change his mind.

Salman's father had a personal security guard by the name of Mehran who had watched Salman grow up and had come to love him. Mehran approached Salman and began to ask about what had happened. Salman explained to him how he had met Christians and learned about their faith. He longed to join them, but his father did not allow him and locked him up.

Mehran made arrangements to help him escape, and told him that he heard of a Christian caravan that was going to Syria. He managed to get word to their monks and prepare horses for Salman to ride to their caravan in the middle of the night. Mehran did everything he could to allow Salman to embark on his most remarkable spiritual journey.

That caravan was only the beginning of his journey towards finding his faith and ultimately the Holy Prophet (pbuh). Salman moved with the caravan of monks towards Syria. He was initiated within the church and took his vows. But his first experience with one of the monks was not a pleasant one.

The first monk whom he had met in Syria would demand money from the community to feed the poor and orphans, but he would pocket the money and spend it on himself. Salman was disappointed to see a man of God deceiving and stealing from the public in this way. Salman left the monk and began searching for the most knowledgeable and ascetic monks of his era. His travels led him to monasteries across the Levant and Iraq. When he found the most pious monk of a town, he would become a devoted student, studying and worshipping with that monk, until he would pass away. Salman would meet and learn from monk after monk, always seeking their advice on where to find guidance after their deaths. Each monk would recommend another ascetic monk until one of them gave Salman great news.

Salman had been in Damascus for ten years when he met this final monk who told him that there was no real follower of God left on the earth anymore and that God was not being worshipped as He was originally meant to be worshipped. He told him that distortions had gradually crept into the religion and that the faith had been altered. Salman replied to this revelation by asking where he should go to find the right path.

He uttered the prophetic description, "There will be a man who will arise from the land of the Arabs. Jesus (pbuh) spoke of him as the spirit of truth. He will be called al-Sadiq, the honest and he will be known as al-Amin, the trustworthy. He doesn't accept *sadaqah*, charity, but he will accept gifts, and you will see the mark of Prophethood between his shoulders."

Salman felt closer to his final destiny and was overjoyed at the momentous news. He intended to join a caravan that was heading towards Arabia. He finally felt that he was at destiny's door, but little did he know that these caravan owners had secretly conspired to enslave Salman and sell him as a slave. One night, they ambushed Salman and enslaved him. Salman was then sold as a slave to one of the Arabs along the caravan route. Poor Salman was devastated by the turn of events although not by his enslavement. He grieved over the disruption of his journey to the Prophet (pbuh). Imagine the heart wrenching pain at the news that one could not reach one's beloved guide!

Interestingly, the man who bought Salman, instead of going towards Mecca, decided to go towards Medina. Salman had heard this Prophet (pbuh) would be in Mecca, so his sorrow was deep. He almost lost hope that he was ever going to meet this Prophet. He couldn't imagine how the Prophet who was in Mecca, spreading the religion would ever come to Medina.

But Allah (swt) works in mysterious ways, and He had a plan for Salman. Salman was eventually sold to a Jewish merchant by the name of Uthman ibn Ashhel who put Salman to work in the orchards. Salman was often high up the palm trees harvesting dates. One day, while high in the treetops he heard Uthman ibn Ashhel speaking with his nephew saying, "May God curse the sons of Khazraj, for that tribe has accepted this man coming from Mecca to Medina by the name of Muhammad (pbuh). He is right now at Quba."

When Salman heard the name of the Holy Prophet (pbuh) his heart leapt with boundless joy and his limbs were shaking; he very nearly fell upon his master, Uthman ibn Ashhel, from the heights of the tree. All of this time he thought the Holy Prophet (pbuh) would be in Mecca and he wouldn't find him because of his enslavement, but Allah had a plan to bring him to his spiritual Master.

The Holy Prophet (pbuh) finally entered Medina. When Salman heard the news, he eventually made his way to the house of Abu Ayyub al-Ansari. Salman took some food with him that he intended to offer as *sadaqah* as well as some food as a gift. Salman intended to ask the Holy Prophet (pbuh) if he would allow him to see the mark of Prophethood between his shoulders. When Salman entered, the Holy Prophet (pbuh) received him magnanimously and asked him to introduce himself and tell him his story.

He introduced himself as Ruzbeh and began with his story of how he was born into a prominent and wealthy Zoroastrian family, how he struggled to seek Christianity, his years as a simple and devoted monk, his travels to Syria, to Mosul, and finally his years in Medina as a slave.

The followers of the Ahl al-Bayt (as) today struggle with implementing even the basics of the religion without having experienced the years and years of hardship and difficulty of this devoted Salman. We should all take a lesson from Salman.

Salman then asked the Holy Prophet (pbuh), "What are your titles?"

The Prophet (pbuh) replied, "al-Sadiq and al-Amin." At this point, Salman offered him and the Companions the food he brought as charity since they were travellers from afar. The Holy Prophet (as) declined the offer of charity, but the others were welcome to eat.

Then Salman offered the food that he brought as a gift and the Noble Messenger (pbuh) said "Bismillah" and ate from it. Eventually, the Prophet gave Salman permission to look at the mark of Prophethood between his shoulders. Salman realised all of the criteria of the prophecy were fulfilled. At this awareness, he submitted to the Divine Religion and said, "I testify that there is no god but God and Muhammad (pbuh) is his Messenger."

The Holy Prophet (pbuh) said, "And I would like to do something as well. Your name is Ruzbeh, but I will change it to Salman. From now on, you will be called Salman." This gift of a new name was like the final initiation into the Divine path, for his name was a derivative of *salam*, peace and blessings, and what a fitting gift for such a momentous journey. But Salman had one major obstacle: he was still an indebted slave.

The Holy Prophet (pbuh) promised to release him from bondage, but Uthman ibn Ashhel would not release him so easily. All around him, Uthman saw how the power of previously influential tribes like the Banu Qaynuqa, Banu Nadhir, and his own tribe, the Banu Qurayza, were losing their power in Medina. Rather than favouring tribal alliances and those with wealth, the Prophet created a new social contract, where citizens piously and equally served each other under God. Uthman wasn't going to acquiesce to this new leader's request so easily and he intended to be extra difficult.

When he was asked how much he wanted for Salman's freedom, he replied with the outrageous request that he wanted three hundred date palm trees planted in his name and forty ounces of gold.

The Holy Prophet (pbuh) looked around at his Companions and asked, "Which one of you will help Salman?"

The offers of help began rolling in like an auction, twenty dirhams from one Companion, thirty from another, forty from yet another, and so on. The generosity of the early Companions of the Holy Prophet (pbuh) was extraordinary. To ensure the religion flourished, they were willing to sacrifice their property and themselves.

When all the date palm trees had been pledged, the Holy Prophet (pbuh) offered to provide the forty ounces of gold. Salman reports that he personally dug every one of the holes for the trees and that the Holy Prophet (pbuh) helped to plant each and every one of them, and not a single sapling perished or dried out.

Eventually Salman was freed and became a loyal Companion of the Holy Prophet (pbuh). His first opportunity to protect the religion came at the Battle of Khandaq. The very name of this battle is due to Salman's idea of digging the trench and he proved himself an excellent military strategist.

Salman came to the Holy Prophet (pbuh) and asked permission to suggest an idea for dealing with the large number of soldiers in the opposition. The army of Abu Sufyan led by Amr ibn Abd al-Wud al-Amri was expected to have ten thousand soldiers who were a renowned force. The Holy Prophet (pbuh) did not have the manpower to counteract them, so strategy was their best weapon.

Salman suggested, "Oh Holy Prophet (pbuh), in my days in Persia, I used to remember wars with the Romans where we would dig a big trench to surround our area, which would make it extra difficult for the horses to cross over. I suggest that what we do the same and dig a trench."

The Holy Prophet (pbuh) was not a leader who ignored his people's suggestions, so long as it was not contradictory to a specific divine command. The Holy Prophet (pbuh) welcomed his idea and alongside his Companions started digging the trench. Another Companion, Ammar ibn Yasir, offered valuable assistance that day in the digging. When the troops approached, Amr ibn Abd al-Wud al-Amri found it extremely difficult to cross over, but eventually he made it across to confront the Muslims.

Amr was not a lightweight in the world of combat, and in fact, his soldiers claimed he enjoyed wrestling lions and wild animals. He called out his challenge, "Oh army of Muhammad (pbuh), if you claim to believe in a heaven, why don't you come out and fight me one-on-one? If you kill me, you will go to that heaven! And if I kill you, you are going to go to that heaven. So why are you so scared to come out and fight?"

What he did not know at that moment was that the Holy Prophet (pbuh) had a young man behind him begging to go forward and fight him. But three times the Holy Prophet (pbuh) had to tell him to sit down because he wanted to see the elder soldiers' response. None came forward. Eventually, the twenty-eight year old Imam Ali (as) was given permission to face Amr ibn Abd al-Wud al-Amri. Imam Ali galloped out to face Amr and answered that he was willing to fight him. Amr asked him to name himself, and he told him he was Ali, the son of Abu Talib.

His opponent refused to fight him because his father, Abu Talib, had once been his friend. Imam Ali's (as) response was bold and clear, "I will fight you (nonetheless), because you are an enemy of Allah (swt)." The fight began, and Amr was overtaken and fell to the ground. All witnessed Imam Ali (as) walk away before coming back to his enemy and finishing him. When he returned to the group of soldiers he called out, "*Allahu Akbar* (God is great)."

The Companions were wondering what happened out there. Imam Ali (as) informed them that as he was about to strike him, Amr spat in his face. Since Ali did not want his last stroke of the sword to be out of personal anger, he walked away. Ali only struck a person who angered Allah (swt). Every act of Imam Ali (as) was purely for the cause of Allah (swt). Back at the opposition's camp, Amr's sister was sitting in the tent amongst others and enjoying a barbeque in a celebratory mood in front of a big bonfire. No one there had the slightest doubt that her brother would return victorious. But the news came that her brother had just been killed, and she was incredulous.

She asked which lion killed him and requested to be brought to her brother's body. They said to her that it was Ali (as), son of Abu Talib, but she had never heard of him. As she went to see the body, like any sister would do, she began to cry and lament. Eventually, she stood up with a smile and declared that she was honoured that the son of Abu Talib killed her brother. Now the incredulity was on the faces of the Holy Prophet's (pbuh) soldiers. She explained that before her brother ever fought anyone he made a special request. Amr always asked his opponent to preserve the ancestral family shield and armour on his body in case he was killed. Amr did not wish to be left nude on the battlefield and dishonoured. She declared that the son of Abu Talib (as) was a noble man, because if he had been shameless and arrogant, he would have taken the shield and plundered her brother's armour. But Ali looked after her brother's request and did not disrobe his body.

At the conclusion of the battle everyone considered Salman and Ali (as) to be the main reasons for the victory. The identity of Ali (as) was well known, he was from the Banu Hashim and from the Ahl al-Bayt (as), but the people wanted to know about Salman. To which tribe did he belong? The Muhajirun came forward and claimed that

Salman was from them. The Ansar did likewise claiming him for themselves. But the Holy Prophet (pbuh) came forward and said, "He is from us, the Ahl al-Bayt (as) , the family of the house." The sixth Imam (as) has a *hadith*, "Never should you say Salman al-Farsi. You must call him Salman al-Muhammadi, because Salman is one of us, the Ahl al-Bayt (as)." The history of the religion of Islam demonstrates that one may be the son of a prophet like the son of Nuh (as), Noah, but you end up dying as an unbeliever, and you may be the son of an unbeliever like Salman, but you end up dying as a member of Aal Muhammad (as). That means this religion is open for anyone to reach the highest levels. The Holy Prophet (pbuh) went a step further in his praise of Salman by saying, "Islam has ten levels of faith. Salman is on the tenth."

The rank that the Prophet (pbuh) attributed to Salman was so esteemed and prominent that it only gives credence to the intimate relationship they must have shared. Salman had such a familial closeness to the Holy Prophet (pbuh) that some narrations even mention that the only men from the Companions who could see the face of Fatimah al-Zahra (as) were Salman and Jabir ibn Abdullah al-Ansari.

Salman himself narrated about the love, care, and devotion he observed in the house of revelation. He described a time when Imam Ali (as) was taking care of Fatimah al-Zahra (as) during a time in which she was ill. He asked her if he could get her something that would make her feel better. She replied, "Just one pomegranate."

When Imam Ali (as) went to buy the pomegranate he came across an old lady who looked ill.

Imam Ali (as) offered her half of the pomegranate and returned to Fatimah al-Zahra (as) with the other half. She thanked him asking Allah (swt) to reward him for helping the old lady. The Holy Prophet (pbuh) sent Salman to their home later and he said that the Holy Prophet (pbuh) heard of Imam Ali's (as) action and he wanted to honour him with nine pomegranates for his good deed.

Imam Ali (as) was confused, that gift wouldn't be from the Holy Prophet (pbuh) because the Holy Prophet (pbuh) had said for every good deed the recompense is ten. Salman smiled and confirmed that indeed Imam Ali (as) knew the Prophet Muhammad (pbuh) better than anyone else. Salman revealed he had taken one out one to see if the Imam (as) would notice.

This narration paints a picture of such a pleasant and personal connection between Salman and Imam Ali (as), yet the level, position, and spiritual depth of Imam Ali (as) was quite unfathomable to even these incredibly close and loyal Companions. There is a narration about Salman entering a gathering where the Holy Prophet (pbuh) was sitting with three individuals and Imam Ali (as). As Salman entered, he met Abu Dhar who was exiting.

Salman inquired who was present there and he named the three individuals but said he did not know the fourth. As he entered and saw that the fourth was Imam Ali (as) he was perplexed. He mentioned this to the Holy Prophet (pbuh) who told him to go and speak to Abu Dhar, which he did. Abu Dhar said to him, "Salman, who truly knows Imam Ali ibn Abi Talib (as)? I haven't come to the understanding of Ali ibn Abi Talib (as)."

Salman, Abu Dhar, and other loyal Companions remained by the side of Imam Ali (as) at Saqifa. When Saqifa occurred after the Holy Prophet (pbuh) passed away, Salman was one of those Companions with Imam Ali (as) and Fatimah al-Zahra (as) when authorities raided their home. Salman was one of the five who shaved their heads to demonstrate their allegiance to Imam Ali (as). Salman is the one who supported Fatimah al-Zahra (as) when she saw Imam Ali (as) taken from their home and she had the right to invoke Allah's punishment upon the aggressors.

The words she used with Salman showed their familial-like connection, "Oh uncle Salman, look at the way they have treated him." Later she would say, "Oh Ali (as), do not allow anyone to come to my funeral, *janazah*, but allow Salman to be there, because Salman is like an uncle to me."

Salman was there at Lady Fatimah's funeral and burial in the night because he was a supporter of the daughter of his beloved Holy Prophet (pbuh) and a disciple of Imam Ali (as). The death of Fatimah al-Zahra (as) caused him much grief because it was as if he had lost his daughter as well.

Later, when Salman was appointed as the governor of Mada'in in Iraq, the people were expecting an important individual to arrive with pomp and ceremony indicating his great status. Instead they saw a man carrying a small bag with a water flask in his hands wearing plain and simple clothing. When he arrived the people of the city asked him who he was and were surprised when he said, "I am the governor." He came as a humble servant of Allah (swt) and the family of the Holy Prophet (pbuh). He came to that position to remind the people that Islam was a religion of modesty and humility.

There is a narration that exemplifies the humility and generosity of Salman. One day, he was walking in the street when a visitor to the city saw him and asked him to pick up his luggage and be his porter, which Salman did. People in the city began to pass by them and were stunned. They asked the visitor if he realised who was carrying his luggage, but he replied that he did not know. They promptly informed him that it was Salman al-Muhammadi, the governor of Mada'in. The visitor immediately begged forgiveness at his disrespect, but Salman said it was his honour to serve the people and continued to help him until he saw him off.

Salman embodied a completely Islamic identity and upheld the principles of Islam. Not only that, but he was an incredible scholar of the religion. He was even one of the first scholars of comparative religion as a Muslim who possessed extensive knowledge of Christian and Zoroastrian scripture and practice. In fact, he was also the first to translate portions of the Holy Qur'an into another language, Persian.

He was considered by many to be overflowing with religious knowledge and insightful wisdom. It is reported the Holy Prophet (pbuh) used to say, "Salman's wisdom is even greater than that of Luqman." Because of his wisdom, the Holy Prophet (pbuh) chose him to be the brother of a famous ascetic, Abu Darda, when the great pact of brotherhood was made in Medina. The Holy Prophet (pbuh) wished to show the difference between simplicity and neglect.

Salman one day saw Abu Darda's wife wearing shabby clothing. He began talking with her to ensure that she was okay. He found out that her husband had renounced the world completely and no longer took any pleasure in anything related to the world. It seems he came to believe that not taking care of his appearance nor looking after his wife's needs was the ultimate religiosity. The Imams of the Ahl al-Bayt (as) on the contrary, despite their lack of desire for worldly possessions, took care of their families and made sure to have a clean and beautiful appearance demonstrating honour and dignity.

Salman sought out his brother Abu Darda and invited him to eat, to which he replied that he was fasting as much as possible. Salman insisted that he come and eat with him, which he did quite voraciously. Then Salman invited him to retire to their quarters to sleep because it was late at night, but Abu Darda said he was staying up the whole night to pray. Again Salman insisted, and he followed him to rest.

Finally Salman reminded him, "O Abu Darda, your Lord has a right over you. Your family has a right over you and your body has a right over you. Give to each their due." He reminded him of the example of the Holy Prophet (pbuh) who looked after himself and looked after the needs of his family and wives. Salman succeeded in correcting Abu Darda by reminding him of the balance and justice within the religion.

Indeed one finds that Salman al-Muhammadi was a man who was able to protect the message of Islam, the example of the Holy Prophet (pbuh), and the legacy of the Holy Imams (as). He embarked on a remarkable journey of the spirit and arrived at the most satisfying end, a member of the beloved Household (as) honoured by Allah (swt).

He was the prime example of someone who achieved a true Islamic identity, shedding all false notions of the self, he was "Salman, the son of Islam from the children of Adam." Salman was one of the greatest Companions who journeyed for years solitarily through many hardships, many religious paths, slavery, disappointments, battles, and political conflicts. Always in pursuit of the truthful path, he ended his journey the way he began: alone.

When he died there was no one to look after him, except Aal Muhammad (as) to honour him and take care of his burial. Of the miracles that Allah (swt) gave Salman was allowing Aal Muhammad (as) to be those who led his final prayers and put to rest the one who had journeyed so long.

Works Cited

Mutahhari, Murtaza. *Fundamentals of Islamic Thought: God, Man and the Universe.* Trans. R. Campbell. (Berkeley, Mizan Press: 1985).

DR. SAYED AMMAR NAKSHAWANI

Chapter 2:

Bilal al-Habashi

Bilal al-Habashi occupies a prominent position within the religion of Islam. He is revered as one of the greatest Companions of both the Holy Prophet (pbuh) and of Imam Ali (as). This man exhibited passion, valour, loyalty and dedication towards the message of the religion of Islam.

His courageous and noble biography has unfortunately been underestimated, and indeed, undervalued. Bilal unquestionably is revered as one of the greatest Companions within the school of Ahl al-Bayt (as) despite the misconception that this school in Islam only reveres the family of the Holy Prophet (pbuh).

Of course, this school fundamentally holds itself to the saying of the Prophet Muhammad (pbuh) regarding the two weighty things, "I leave behind for you the Qur'an and my Ahl al-Bayt (as)." As a secondary principle, the school of Ahl al-Bayt (as) judges any Companion of the Holy Prophet (pbuh) as the Qur'an judges him. There are certain Companions whom the Qur'an discusses and reveres very highly. For example, the following verse in the Qur'an beautifully describes the positive attributes of the Companions:

Muhammad is the Messenger of God; and those with him are forceful against the disbelievers, merciful among themselves. You see them bowing and prostrating, seeking bounty from God and

[His] pleasure. Their mark is on their faces from the trace of prostration...(Q48:29).

Likewise, there are verses that distinguish very clearly between the manifest, public behaviour and the inner, private beliefs of some Companions. It is critical to note that Allah (swt) makes this important distinction quite sternly declaring the extent of the hypocrisy of some Companions. Thus, the Qur'an states:

And among those around you of the Bedouins are hypocrites, and [also] from the people of Medina. They have become quite stern in their hypocrisy. You, [O Muhammad], do not know them, [but] We know them. We will punish them twice...(Q9:101).

In the Islamic tradition, there are many methodologies to analysing the Companions. The school of Ahl al-Bayt (as) does so by comparing each Companion's merits and conduct during the lifetime of the Holy Prophet (pbuh) to his life after the Holy Prophet's death. If he continued living upon virtuous principles, then respect is granted. However, if an individual displayed conduct that saddened the Holy Prophet (pbuh) in his lifetime or began to behave inappropriately after the Holy Prophet's death, then the merits of that person are open to analysis.

Bilal al-Habashi's biography begins with the story of the Year of the Elephant, Aam al-Fil, a year that was significant in more ways than one. First, the Holy Prophet (pbuh) was born in that year.

Second, an invasion of Mecca occurred that year and is discussed in Chapter 105 of the Holy Qur'an, entitled The Elephant.

The King of Yemen, Abraha, was the former viceroy of the Aksum kingdom. He had risen to power and built a grand cathedral in his zeal for the promotion of Christianity and probably for control of the lucrative pilgrimage profits in the region. He had taken an army towards Mecca intending to destroy the Ka'ba, in the hopes that the Meccan pilgrims would come to him and his cathedral instead. His grand scheme seemed plausible with his massive army and strong, impenetrable elephants leading the way.

In his advancement towards the Ka'ba he met Abdul Muttalib, the grandfather of the Holy Prophet (pbuh) who approached him asking for his stolen camels to be returned. Abraha was in shock that this nobleman was not trembling in fear of the imminent military threat, but was instead preoccupied with his herd. "Do you not care about protecting the Ka'ba?" Abraha asked.

Abdul Muttalib confidently answered Abraha, "The Ka'ba has its own Protector, and I am the protector of my camels."

When Abraha advanced towards the Ka'ba, the narrations state that an attack of flying birds hailed stones upon him and his soldiers ultimately defeating them. The Qur'an says:

> In the name of Allah, the Beneficent, the Merciful.
> Seest thou not how thy Lord dealt with the
> Companions of the Elephant? Did He not make their
> treacherous plan go astray? And He sent against them

Flights of Birds, Striking them with stones of baked clay. Then did He make them like an empty field of stalks and straw, (of which the corn) has been eaten up. (Q105:1-5)

When Abraha was defeated, he left behind his sister and her daughter by the name of Jumanah. The Khazamites caught Jumanah and then sold her off to Banu Jumah. The chief of that tribe, by the name of Khalaf, or Kalaf in some narrations, ordered that she should be under the custody of one of his personal slaves known as Rabah.

This Rabah had a particular honour as the caretaker of the idols in the Ka'ba itself. Eventually he married Jumanah and they had two sons and a daughter. The eldest son was called Bilal. The second son was named Khalid and the daughter named Ghusrah. Hence, Bilal al-Habashi's mother is the niece of Abraha, who attempted to attack the Ka'ba.

The narrations state that Bilal lived in prosperity because of his role within the Banu Jumah even though his father was a slave. When Khalaf died, his son Umayyah, became the head of the tribe. When Rabah died, his son Bilal became the custodian of the Ka'ba and the idols.

Bilal's master Umayyah was known as an enemy of the Holy Prophet (pbuh). As one of the aristocrats of Arabia he was amongst the elite who did not want to lose their position, status or wealth when the Holy Prophet (pbuh) began to preach the message of Islam. Amongst Umayyah's peers and compatriots in defiance of the message of Islam was Abu Sufyan, Walid ibn Mughirah, and Utbah ibn Rabi'a.

In fact, Umayyah ibn Khalaf was the person who challenged the Prophet on the concept of resurrection when the following verse of Sura Ya Sin was revealed:

And he makes comparisons for Us, and forgets his own (origin and) Creation: He says, "Who can give life to (dry) bones and decomposed ones (at that)?" Say, "He will give them life Who created them for the first time! for He is Well-versed in every kind of creation" (Q36:78-79).

Whereas this Umayyah would be incredulous about the power of the One God and ask such a question, Bilal would question the worship of the idols despite being given the honourable position of caretaker. Perhaps by the very virtue that these lifeless stones needed a human caretaker, Bilal began to question their authenticity.

He wondered at their defencelessness and thought that had he desired he could crack them in half himself; clearly he doubted the idols divinity.

The narrations state that the young Bilal was close friends with Ammar ibn Yasir. One day he saw Ammar bound and being dragged by a group of people and Bilal was shocked. He asked his master Umayyah what was going on and why Ammar was being taken. He found out that Ammar had declared his belief in Islam, a new religion that Muhammad (pbuh) was beginning to preach.

Bilal knew the character of the Holy Prophet (pbuh) as al-Sadiq and al-Amin, the truthful and the trustworthy, as did the community. Umayyah mockingly said that this religion believed that a black man was equal to a white man. He scoffed at the unconventional notion that his own slave had the same status as him in the eyes of a God. But Bilal wasn't laughing; for the first time, someone had openly declared his worth as a human being; for the first time, someone honoured him regardless of his skin colour.

He heard that the religion taught that women and men were equal in their worth before God. Muhammad (pbuh) taught that there would be a reckoning for life on earth called the Day of Judgment and the Day of Resurrection.

Bilal was charged with energy and full of questions, so he sought out the Holy Prophet (pbuh). The Holy Prophet (pbuh) informed him of the religion, but told him to keep his religiosity quiet. Later, after his encounter with Muhammad (pbuh) the narrations say that Bilal went to the Ka'ba and stood before the idol Hubal lamenting that he ever considered the man-made statues gods.

Believing to be alone, Bilal spat at Hubal to show his disgust. But there was someone who happened to be spying on Bilal, watching his moves and seeing if he was among those influenced by Muhammad (pbuh). While Bilal made his way to the house of Umayyah and to his small room, the spy who had followed him there went directly to Umayyah to reveal all he saw. Umayyah flew into a rage disparaging Bilal for betraying his protection and his position.

But Umayyah's anger reached its peak when Umm Jamil the sister of Abu Sufyan and wife of Abu Lahab denied him entry into the parliament, Dar al-Nadwah. As a leader within the parliament, she proclaimed that any member of Muhammad's (pbuh) tribe as well as anyone whose relative joined the religion of Muhammad (pbuh) was forbidden to enter and participate in the parliament.

She informed Umayyah that Bilal was amongst those that had joined the religion, and at that he left seething with anger and humiliation. He returned home and began screaming wildly for Bilal to be brought to him. He demanded to know if what he heard was true, and Bilal admitted that the religion of Islam had indeed freed him from oppression and that all men were equal. Umayyah wouldn't dare be put down by his slave and be told what to do by his inferior. He had him tied up and beaten; and thus began the extreme abuse of Bilal ibn Rabah.

Umayyah had Bilal dragged to the centre of the city in the scorching heat, torturing him with fire and earth. His skin was seared, yet he still proclaimed the oneness of Allah. His eyes were blood-shot and dazed, but he looked towards the heavens proclaiming the oneness of Allah.

Umayyah ordered two of his slaves to put Bilal on the ground, and he began to whip him profusely, over and over. But Bilal would reply, "There is only one God. There is only one God. There is only one God." Umayyah told him to say Hubal was the god, but Bilal continued his refrain of "*Ahad, Ahad, Ahad*", One, One, One. The torture continued for days and Bilal's naked body was flung upon the burning sands and put beneath a massive black rock. But his voice continued to call out, "*Ahad, Ahad, Ahad*".

The news of Bilal becoming Muslim was now all over the city, and Umayyah was having nightmares about it. Umayyah escalated the severe torture in his attempt to gain back control and to put down this religion. He chained Bilal this time near the pens of the animals, and ordered the children to stone him. Bilal was being pelted with stones for his belief in the oneness of God and love for the Holy Prophet (pbuh).

He was pelted and tortured in the cruellest of ways that even Amr ibn al-Aas (infamous for the cruelty he displays toward the body of Muhammad b. Abi Bakr) took pity on him although he had not yet converted himself. Amr narrates that when he walked past Bilal, he saw how much he was being hurt that he told Umayyah, "Surely you have tortured the man enough." But this intervention did not relieve Bilal from the abuse. It was only when the Holy Prophet (pbuh) ransomed Bilal that he was finally freed.

The Holy Prophet (pbuh) sent Abu Bakr with five ounces of gold to ransom Bilal. The narrations state that Bilal was relieved from the abuse, so he immediately joined the Holy Prophet (pbuh) and eventually migrated to Medina. When they entered Medina, the attack on the Muslims continued now in the form of regular skirmishes and attacks at the boundaries of the city. For two years,

Abu Sufyan and Abu Jahl would not cease attacking the outskirts of Medina.

They were determined to kill Muhammad (pbuh) and put a stop to his movement, but at each and every turn they could not stop him. At the Hijrah (migration), their assassination plot in the night failed and every other attack missed Muhammad (pbuh).

Finally, in the second year after Hijrah, they escalated the attacks against the Holy Prophet (pbuh) by setting up the pretext for a full out battle. The Battle of Badr began with Abu Sufyan's inflammatory rumour that Muhammad (pbuh) had attacked his caravan. The Meccan elite, eager for a reason to fight Muhammad (pbuh), was ready to amass troops and launch an offensive. Abu Jahl began the effort by raising over nine hundred and fifty soldiers. Umayyah, who at the beginning of the announcement of Prophecy was a staunch enemy of the Holy Prophet (pbuh) and the one who had tortured Bilal all those years in Mecca, was found lingering behind during this battle because he had heard that his life was in danger. One of his companions told him to take kohl, black eyeliner that the women wear, and put it on. Umayyah, humiliated, made his way to the battle.

Approaching the battlefield that day, Abu Jahl remarked arrogantly that there was no possible way that Muhammad's (pbuh) three hundred and thirteen soldiers could defeat his army. He underestimated the young Ali ibn Abi Talib (as) who was the backbone of the Holy Prophet (pbuh) in that army. The narrations state that Ali ibn Abi Talib (as) on that day demolished the army of the opposition; of the seventy of their leaders that were killed, thirty-five of them fell from the strike of Ali ibn Abi Talib (as).

Bilal was successful in fighting the enemies as well. The torturer Umayyah, now a lumbering, overweight man, who had shown no mercy to the innocent Bilal, was cornered. Abdul Rahman ibn Awf, a Muslim fighting on the side of the Prophet (pbuh), tried to protect his old friend Umayyah, even though he was on the opposing side. But Umayyah could not escape and Bilal finally struck the source of his many years of oppression; he slew Umayyah and avenged himself on the day of Badr.

Later that year, after this significant battle, the Holy Prophet (pbuh) began to reveal new principles and practices of the religion. The practice of ritual prayer, (*salah*) was introduced. Medina was the city in which the new Muslims began to perform the acts of worship, therefore, verses revealed in Medina were both instructional and societal. Now that the Holy Prophet (pbuh) began to institute the *salah*, the next issue that arose was the method of congregating the community for the appointed time of worship. Some narrations state that the Companions discussed amongst themselves a number of possibilities, such as ringing a bell or lighting a fire, in addition to other ideas.

In other schools of Islam it is reported that the call to prayer, the *adhan*, came from a man named Abdullah ibn Zayd ibn Abd Rabbihi, who allegedly had a dream regarding the method of the call to prayer. He is reported to have suggested that the declaration of belief in One God, His greatness, and the prophethood of Muhammad should be recited aloud to call people to prayer, whereupon the Holy Prophet (pbuh) agreed to his suggestion.

The school of Ahl al-Bayt (as) differs in their view on how the *adhan* originated specifically because the originator of this *hadith*, or narration, Abdullah ibn Zayd ibn Abd Rabbihi, is not known in any other context except via another narration that describes his daughter's petition to a later caliph. Umar ibn Abdul Aziz, an Umayyad caliph who abolished the cursing of Imam Ali (as), is reported to have received his daughter when she came asking for money from the treasury because her father fought in the Battle of Uhud. It is significant that she doesn't mention anything about her father originating the *adhan*.

Furthermore and more importantly, Bukhari and Muslim don't mention him as the originator of the *adhan*. According to the traditions of the Ahl al-Bayt (as), the *adhan* came from Allah (swt) to the Holy Prophet (pbuh) who then directed Bilal to take on this monumental role.

Amongst the people, a buzz could be heard before the reciter was revealed. The crowds were murmuring, "Who will it be?" Certainly a few noses would be upturned and egos bruised when the announcement was made. Indeed no sooner had Bilal appeared and recited, did the first hateful racist words dampen the expectant mood. One of the Arabs, who used to despise the Holy Prophet (pbuh) said,

"Muhammad (pbuh) is using his black crow to recite the *adhan* for us."

The Holy Prophet (pbuh) eradicated racism and tribalism at every turn by bringing towards himself individuals from all different ethnicities. For example, Salman was from Persia, Bilal was from Abyssinia, Ammar's family was originally from Yemen, and there were even others from Rome. This was a historic move to have one of the Companions who was once looked down upon by everyone, who was tortured beneath a rock, to now stand above everyone and call them all to worship shoulder to shoulder.

Without a doubt this action signalled a remarkable change of events and a major paradigm shift. Unfortunately, this fundamental message of Islam and the living example of inclusion demonstrated by the Holy Prophet (pbuh) is utterly ignored today. The persistence of the belief in racial and ethnic superiority within the Muslim community today is a disease that seems resistant to a remedy.

Some reports mention that when Bilal recited the call to prayer in Arabic, he could not pronounce the letter "*sheen*" properly, and instead would say "*seen*"; Bilal said "*as-hadu*" instead of "*ash-hadu*", meaning "I testify." Now even further criticism was launched against him. He was ridiculed, and of course, this was a criticism of the Holy Prophet's (pbuh) decision as well.

The Holy Prophet (pbuh) replied, "The "*seen*" of Bilal is "*sheen*" in the eyes of Allah (swt)". Furthermore, he favoured his *adhan* and would personally request him to recite saying, "Bilal, please me with your *adhan*." Clearly the Holy Prophet (pbuh) valued Bilal's service and elevated his status in the eyes of the community by granting him this noble position.

Even Imam Zayn al-Abidin (as) in "Risalat al-Huquq", "The Treatise of Rights", extols the rights of the *muadhin*, or the caller to prayer, "The right of the *muadhin* is that you know that he is reminding you of your Lord, calling you to your good fortune, and helping you to accomplish what God has made obligatory upon you. So thank him for that just as you thank one who does good to you".

Bilal's role was not only as the *muadhin* of the Holy Prophet (pbuh), but as the first treasurer of Islam as well. Bilal al-Habashi, a former slave, was honoured with the prodigious responsibility of managing the Bayt al-Maal, the treasury in an Islamic state, designated for the orphans, the needy, and the widows. He was so trusted and reliable that the Holy Prophet (pbuh) was certain he would ensure its wealth was distributed properly.

In the city of Medina, his life and status vastly improved. Nevertheless, his love and devotion to the Holy Prophet (pbuh) continually increased, and he did not puff himself up in arrogant pride. He himself composed lines of poetry where he described about how much he revered the Holy Prophet (pbuh), "When we look for morals, you are the model amongst us." The Holy Prophet (pbuh) used to say, "I love Bilal," and Bilal used to say, "I love the *akhlaq* of the Holy Prophet (pbuh)."

DR. SAYED AMMAR NAKSHAWANI

Bilal was continually learning from the Holy Prophet (pbuh) even after obtaining such distinguished positions. Arrogance and entitlement did not worm their way into his heart. Even at the Battle of Khaybar Bilal received a lesson in *akhlaq*, or behaviour. When the Battle of Khaybar ended and the Muslims were victorious, mainly because of the courage and efforts of Imam Ali (as), the narrations mention that the women of the Jewish community were held as prisoners.

The Holy Prophet (pbuh) asked Bilal to bring them forward and when he went to do so, he took the women through the middle of the battlefield. As soon as the Holy Prophet (pbuh) saw Bilal do this, he put his head down. Bilal was taken aback by his gesture and immediately asked what was wrong, concerned to see his beloved Prophet looking pained. At this point the Holy Prophet (pbuh) expressed disappointment with Bilal's *akhlaq*. Bilal was uncertain about what he had done wrong, and so he asked.

The Holy Prophet (pbuh) replied by pointing out that while they had fought the men of this community, the women should be spared any further pain and Muslims should not hurt them by making them walk past the dead bodies of their husbands. The Holy Prophet even told him that he expected better *akhlaq* from him and thought that he would not do such a thing. Bilal, in all humility, expressed that this was a lesson that he would never forget.

In the following year, when the Holy Prophet (pbuh) returned to Mecca from Medina after eight years, he again sent Bilal to recite the *adhan*, and this time atop the Holy Ka'ba itself. The Meccans who were so elitist and arrogant now witnessed Bilal ibn Rabah al-Habashi stand and recite, "I testify that there is no god but Allah (swt). I testify that Muhammad (pbuh) is the messenger of God." They could not doubt that this religion was for every person after having witnessed the clemency that the Holy Prophet (pbuh) extended to all the Meccans upon their conquest and having heard a former slave of African origin recite the *adhan* for the religion. Bilal was a living example that any human being was welcome to the religion.

The Holy Prophet's forbearance was not the only attribute Bilal had the privilege to observe, but his good nature and humour as well. Bilal narrates that one day he was walking along the street and he came upon an old woman weeping. He inquired after her out of concern, and came to find out that she had had just met the Holy Prophet (pbuh) and had asked the Holy Prophet (pbuh) if she would enter Paradise. He replied regretfully that there would be no old women in Paradise.

Bilal told her not to worry and that he would go and speak to the Holy Prophet (pbuh) directly. When he came upon the Holy Prophet (pbuh) he told him what he had seen and beseeched him to tell her that she will be in Paradise. The Holy Prophet (pbuh) replied to Bilal by telling him that there would be no black person in Paradise either. Now poor Bilal was confused, and he went to Abbas, the uncle of the Holy Prophet (pbuh) and asked him to speak to him for he too now was saddened.

Abbas complied, but got a similar response, that there would be no old men in Paradise as well. Now Abbas was the one who finally demanded to know what he meant. With a smile, the Holy Prophet (pbuh) replied, "When I said there are no old men and women, it is because you are all going to be *shabab*, or youths, in Paradise. When I said there is no one who is black, it means there is no one who will be blackened with sin in Paradise. All of you will have the light of purity in Paradise."

Bilal was enriched spiritually and socially by his connection with the Holy Prophet (pbuh), living in the shade of his pure piety, respect, humility, courage, and good humour amongst so many other noble and divinely inspired traits. All the years of hardship, challenge, and difficulty that Bilal faced alongside the Divine Guide forged an iron-grip of commitment and loyalty. The narrations state that Bilal was the man whom the Holy Prophet ordered to call the dispersing pilgrims back on the scorching hot Day of Ghadir. This Day of Ghadir is the day in which Muslims were not left without a guide; indeed the Muslims were left with a colossus like Ali ibn Abi Talib (as).

He specifically asked Bilal to recite the *adhan* in order for the people to stop. As he began to recite, a murmur arose amongst the crowd; questions were being asked about what was going on. What was the reason for which people were being called back?

After the preparation of a pulpit made of saddles and blankets, the Holy Prophet (pbuh) addressed the crowd in a lengthy speech and raised the hands of Imam Ali (as) with the famous words, "Of whomsoever I am his master, this Ali (as) is also his master."

Often this line is reduced to a declaration of friendship, but what pettiness that definition ascribes to the Holy Prophet (pbuh)! Imagine this utterly cautious, thoughtful, socially sensitive Divine Guide for mankind stopping a massive group of pilgrims in the oppressive heat to announce such a simple statement. That interpretation is the furthest from the truth, most particularly when one understands the length of the Ghadir sermon and the number of times Imam Ali (as) was indicated within it as a successor, leader, and legatee.

Still many historians say that the Holy Prophet (pbuh) only wished to declare Ali (as) to be his friend, and nothing more. Understanding the context is yet another way to clarify the meaning. In Arabic the Holy Prophet (pbuh) said, "...*Al nabiya awla bil mominina.*" The use of the word *mawla* with the word *awla* means that he was saying, "Do I not possess a greater right over the believers?" To which all present replied, "Yes oh Holy Prophet (pbuh)." Then he finished this particular statement with, "Whoever I have mastership over, Ali (as) now possesses it."

Bilal witnessed this whole event and after the Holy Prophet (pbuh) passed away, Bilal was one of the loyal companions of Imam Ali (as) in honour of the Prophet's declaration. He was one of those who adhered to the Holy Prophet's request (pbuh) to honour and protect his family, the Ahl al-Bayt (as). In the historical narrations Ammar, Salman, Abu Dhar, and Miqdad demonstrated their loyalty to Imam Ali (as) and their willingness to join him in fighting for his leadership by arriving with their shaved heads at his house the days after Saqifa.

Bilal's stand against this injustice was that he never recited his *adhan* again after the Holy Prophet (pbuh) died. His complete cut-off is a strong and convincing evidence for his loyalty to the Ahl al-Bayt (as). The only *hadith* that indicates he recited *adhan* was for Fatimah al-Zahra (as) after her personal request and as a comfort to her in her last days; otherwise, no one else ever heard it again.

He highlighted true companionship in that not only was he a Companion of the Holy Prophet (pbuh), but after the Holy Prophet's (pbuh) death, he was respectful of Fatimah al-Zahra (as). He was amongst the few who protected her message and the message of Imam Ali (as).

After the Holy Prophet (pbuh) died, Umar ibn Khatab came and dragged Bilal by his robe demanding from him, "Abu Bakr freed you when you were a slave, and now you don't pay allegiance to him?" Bilal replied, "If he freed me for Allah (swt), then leave it to Allah (swt) to reward him. If he freed me for himself, then I will come to serve him right now. But if he freed me so that I leave the man chosen at Ghadir, that I will not do."

Sheikh Ja'far al-Tusi, in *Ikhtyar al-Rijaal*, mentions that Bilal was a pious follower of Imam Ali (as) and that is why Bilal recited these lines of poetry in reference to the first Caliph Abu Bakr, "By Allah (swt), I did not follow him, and if it wasn't for Allah's (swt) help, they would have stood on my limbs like hyenas. Allah (swt) is vast with goodness. Allah (swt) is vast with honour. You will not find me following innovators, because I am not a man of innovation."

As a consequence of his strong stand against the first two caliphs, they exiled him to Shaam, known today as Damascus, and that is where he is buried. Any rational examiner of history ought to wonder why the *muadhin* of the Holy Prophet (pbuh) is not buried in Medina or in Mecca. He died in Syria seven years after the Holy Prophet (pbuh) died because he was kicked out of his very own community that he had helped forge alongside the Holy Prophet (pbuh).

There is a *hadith* narrated by Imam Ja'far al-Sadiq (as) that says, "May Allah (swt) bless Bilal. He loved us Aal Muhammad (as) and he was one of Allah's (swt) pious servants"; and it was because of his unwavering loyalty that this beloved and close Companion of the Holy Prophet (pbuh) died alone and apart from the Muslim community he sacrificed so much to help establish.

DR. SAYED AMMAR NAKSHAWANI

Chapter 3: Ammar ibn Yasir

Ammar ibn Yasir occupies a prominent position in the religion of Islam as being one of the greatest Companions of the Holy Prophet (pbuh) and Imam Ali (as). He was a man who was revered for his bravery, for his passion, and for his valour. Ammar was a man from whose life many lessons may be learned and many examples may be derived. He was truly a man who remained loyal to the cause of the religion of Islam.

When one examines the life of Ammar ibn Yasir, one finds that whether he was at the age of thirty, or even at the age of ninety-three, every aspect of the life of Ammar ibn Yasir represents a profound commitment towards the religion of Islam. It is extraordinary that at the Battle of Siffin, Ammar ibn Yasir, according to most accounts, was killed at the age of ninety or older. Therefore, he lived a very long life serving the religion of Islam, from the cradle until the grave. Such a steadfast and enduring companion is an extraordinary role model and one can extract many benefits from studying his biography.

First, Ammar is honoured as one of the foremost amongst the *sahabah*, or Companions, of the Holy Prophet (pbuh). The first *sahabah* were no ordinary men. These were people who had the extraordinary privilege and blessing to have walked with the Holy Prophet (pbuh), talked with him, ate with him, drank with him, but also most importantly to have seen the hardest of years alongside the

DR. SAYED AMMAR NAKSHAWANI

Holy Prophet (pbuh). The first to convert in Mecca sacrificed so much in the nascent years of the religion, enduring the loss of parents, their homes, their livelihoods, and even their place of birth.

Many endured years of torture, intimidation, and public ridicule. This loyal, enduring devotion is preserved beautifully in *al-Sahifat al-Sajjadiyah*, also called the "Psalms of Islam", composed by the fourth Imam, Imam Zayn al-Abidin (as). In this first ever prayer manual in Islamic history is a supplication specifically for the *sahabah* of the Holy Prophet (pbuh) praising them for their sacrifices and praying for them to be honoured by God:

> O God, and as for the Companions of Muhammad
> specifically, those who did well in companionship,
> who stood the good test in helping him, responded to
> him when he made them hear his messages'
> argument, separated from mates and children in
> manifesting his word, fought against fathers and sons
> in strengthening his prophecy, and through him
> gained victory; those who were wrapped in affection
> for him,
> hoping for a commerce that comes not to naught in
> love for him; those who were left by their clans when
> they clung to his handhold and denied by their
> kinsfolk
> when they rested in the shadow of his kinship; forget
> not, O God, what they abandoned for Thee and in

Thee, and make them pleased with Thy good pleasure
for the sake of the creatures they drove to Thee while
they were with Thy Messenger, summoners to Thee
for Thee.

Show gratitude to them for leaving the abodes of their
people for Thy sake
and going out from a plentiful livelihood to a narrow
one, and [show gratitude to] those of them who faced
oppression and whom Thou multiplied in exalting
Thy religion.

Clearly the followers of the Ahl al-Bayt (as) revere the noble
Companions without a shadow of doubt and seek to learn lessons
from these individuals.

Second, the study of Ammar ibn Yasir's life inspires courage
and clarity to face one's own trials and tribulations. Clearly next to
these noble Companions' struggles, the issues most contemporary
followers of the Ahl al-Bayt (as) face in Western society pale in
comparison. Ammar ibn Yasir's story is one that is full of peaks and
troughs, one where at times he is smiling and at other times facing
intense pressure to relinquish his faith.

Imam Ali (as) loved Ammar dearly, honouring him as one of his
closest companions. After the assassinations of Ammar (in the Battle
of Siffin) and Malik al-Ashtar, the value of these two was revealed by
Muawiyah who arrogantly claimed, "I have cut the two wings of Ali
ibn Abi Talib (as)."

Ammar ibn Yasir was born in the same year as the Holy Prophet (pbuh), the year of the elephant. Many narrations mention that they were the best of friends throughout their lives. Even in the days when the Holy Prophet (pbuh) hadn't announced his Prophethood, they were close friends. Ammar's father, Yasir, was originally from Yemen. Yasir and his brothers Haarith, Malik, and a third brother went on a journey to Mecca. But this third brother never returned from that journey and after some time, they began to get worried. Yasir and his brothers Malik and Haarith decided to pursue him to see if they could reunite.

It was common in those days for Yemenis to go towards Mecca and Medina to find more profitable work. But unfortunately, when they reached Mecca, their brother was nowhere to be found. Nonetheless, Yasir decided to stay in Mecca even though he did not have any relatives in the city. If one didn't have family in a particular city, one would need to align with one of the local tribes. Once a relationship was established, an individual could begin to work for that tribe.

Yasir aligned himself with the head of Banu Makhzum, Abu Hudhayfah al-Makhzumi. This famous tribe in Mecca included many prominent Arabians, for example, Khalid ibn Walid and his father Walid ibn Mughirah, as well as Abu Jahl. One side of Umar ibn Khattab's family was Makhzumi. Yasir also ended up marrying a lady by the name of Sumayyah bint Khayal who was a servant of Banu Makhzum, and Ammar was their first child.

When Ammar was young many of the narrations indicate that he was very quiet and that one would hardly hear his voice. His silence caused some people to believe he wasn't very intelligent. However, they later realised Ammar was, in fact, a deep thinker. He used to ponder often about the way he was living and about the society around him. The Holy Prophet (pbuh) said, "An hour of reflection is greater than seventy years of worship."

Within the contemporary Western world, the pace of life is so rapid, that this attitude of reflection that Ammar exemplified would do many people good. The examination of the quality and habits of one's life, in particular, whether religion is a priority is necessary and perhaps even overdue for some. Within Islamic theology, the remembrance of the hereafter refocuses the meaning of life and the actions within it.

Ammar at a young age would sit with his father questioning and reflecting on the behaviour of those around him. He found the way the Arab tribes behaved to be deplorable: all the rampant backbiting and gossiping, lawlessness, war-mongering, mistreatment of women, and burial of their daughters alive. His father would discourage him from voicing his displeasure, reminding his son of their status as servants within a well-known tribe. Ammar would even complain to his father that he could not respect the Ka'ba by bowing down to idols that they themselves could break. His father told him that the Ka'ba has a Lord that will protect it, and went on to tell him of the story of Abraha, the priest from Yemen that had come to try and attack the Ka'ba in the year Ammar was born. Allah (swt) sent birds that pelted and destroyed the troops of Abraha.

Some say his father Yasir was a monotheist, others say he was uncertain in his beliefs; nevertheless, he would sit with his son Ammar often in reflection and discussion. His father would always tell him to look towards the noble tribe of Banu Hashim as exemplars. He would describe how the young Muhammad (pbuh) of this tribe was someone whose character was the best of characters.

On one occasion during their discussions, there was an incident of remarkable injustice. A man who had come to trade went to the top of Mount Abu Qubays, one of the biggest mountains in Arabia, and cried out to the people and complained that his goods had been stolen and pleaded for someone to stand up for him. Ammar asked his father what was going on and he replied by explaining the lack of security for traders who visited Mecca. They traded at great risk of being cheated or looted en route.

There was no governing body to whom one could appeal for grievances. In this case, a man from the Zubaydi tribe came with his goods to trade and al-Aas ibn Wa'il, the father of Amr ibn al-Aas, took the goods, and wouldn't pay the man the money. The Zubaydi man tried to negotiate, but al-Aas refused and started threatening him.

Ammar noticed that there was a man by the name of Usayd, the brother of Khadijah (as) who along with the Holy Prophet (pbuh) formed the group called Hilf al-Fudhul, The League of Justice. The

Holy Prophet (pbuh) was only twenty years old at the time and he was working towards the betterment of his society via this group to ensure the just treatment of traders, travellers, and members of the community.

Ammar was deeply impressed by this effort of reform and change, and in this case, the Zubaydi man did get his goods back through the work of The League of Justice. In another incident, a man by the name of Nabi'a ibn Hajjaj pressured and intimidated a local family to take their daughter, by the name of Qatool, for his pleasure. Naturally, the family refused and pleaded for the safety of their daughter.

The League of Justice stepped in and protected the daughter. Additionally, there was a man by the name of Harb ibn Umayyah who had killed someone and The League of Justice stepped in and ensured justice was served.

The narrations recount from Ammar himself how deeply he was moved by this impetus for justice and reform. From his youth he became encouraged and inspired by his friend Muhammad (pbuh). When at the age of forty he came forward and announced his Prophethood, Ammar could think of nothing else but how to reach out to the Holy Prophet (pbuh) and tell him that he wanted to join his path. But coming out in the open was difficult, if not outright dangerous.

Ammar was still aligned to a tribe, Banu Makhzum, which detested the Holy Prophet (pbuh). Ammar would face the risk of being executed or at a minimum harassed and tortured. Reports narrate that Ammar went to key people to inquire about the Prophet's location, and he found out that he was at the house called Dar al-Arqam. The earliest converts would gather at this house; there he saw Suhayb al-Rumi (the Roman) standing outside.

Both of them were wary of one another, and began to question the reason for each being there. With some trepidation Suhayb admitted that he came to join the religion of Muhammad (pbuh); Ammar was greatly relieved and together they entered the house.

There they saw the Holy Prophet (pbuh) and were immovable in rapt attention till the morning light forced them to leave. These privileged few sat down with this noble and divinely inspired figure as he explained the religion to them and the verses revealed to him by the Archangel Jibreel (Gabriel).

The House of Arqam's exterior did not reveal the depth and glory of what was transpiring in the interior. This was a gathering of a select group of people who could maintain the security of the message and the Prophet's revelations from the Creator of the Universe Himself. The narrations state that Jibreel (on that particular night when Ammar entered) had revealed a verse to the Holy Prophet (pbuh) and the Holy Prophet (pbuh) explained it. Ammar went home that night without realising this revelation would open more eyes to Divine Truth.

As he came home in the early morning hours, Ammar carefully opened the door to his house, and in the dark, his shoulder brushed the idol his family kept in a niche. The lifeless idol fell and broke. When his father heard the clamour and saw what had happened, he was horrified and yelled at his son for accidentally "killing a god." Ammar was perplexed by such a foolish statement and asked his father if he truly realised what he had just said.

He questioned his father about the irony of worshipping a god that he could easily kill himself. At this point, his mother Sumayyah came forward chastising Ammar for speaking disrespectfully to his father and dishonouring the gods. She was taken aback at Ammar's boldness and demanded to know where he learned to speak in this manner. He replied that he had learned to speak this truth from Muhammad (pbuh), the Holy Prophet of God.

Sumayyah inquired about what else Muhammad (pbuh) had taught him. He went on to reveal that he had just come from the House of Arqam where Muhammad (pbuh) had taught the following verse from the Qur'an, "In the name of Allah, the Beneficent, the Merciful. When the female (infant), buried alive, is questioned - For what crime was she killed?" (Q81:8-9).

As soon as Sumayyah heard this, the floodgates of her memory burst open and she began to cry. Ammar was alarmed and apologetic; he asked her why she was crying. She was too overcome to answer, so his father explained that Ammar's mother had two older sisters who were born before her but her grandfather buried both of them alive as newborns. But when the second defenceless girl child was being buried, her small hand touched his beard. This tender, innocent gesture penetrated his hardened heart and he vowed that if he had a third daughter he would keep her alive and cherish her. The third daughter was Sumayyah, Ammar's mother.

Sumayyah wiped her tears and confidently told Ammar, if Muhammad (pbuh) was preaching about a religion that defended the rights of the woman then she and his father intended to join the new followers. So two new converts entered the faith, and what they were to face would be the highest price one could pay for adherence to the message. At the same time, Abu Jahl, the uncle of the Prophet (pbuh) and an aristocrat with much power and sway, began slowly finding out about the growth of the new religious movement. To address this growing subversive movement, Abu Jahl, Abu Sufyan, and Abu Lahab gathered in their parliament, by the name of Dar al-Nadwah, and pressured Abu Talib to advise his nephew to stop preaching and causing unrest. They offered him money, houses, women of beauty and status, and all manner of worldly pleasures to desist.

When Abu Talib told the Holy Prophet (pbuh), he replied with the famous response, "If they gave me the sun in my right hand, and the moon in my left, I would not stop preaching the rights and principles of this religion."

The opponents of Muhammad's (pbuh) message observed more and more people entering the way of Islam. In an effort to stop the tide, the heads of Dar al-Nadwah would ban the leaders of a tribe from entering the parliament if any members of that tribe converted.

Abu Jahl, already an opponent of Muhammad (pbuh), arrived one day and was blocked from entering.

Taken aback, he demanded to know the reason. They told him that Ammar ibn Yasir and his parents were from his tribe and they were followers of Muhammad (pbuh). Abu Jahl could not believe it; he was furious. Immediately, he went towards the public square and made a threatening announcement; every tribal leader who had Muslims in his tribe must torture them to death or execute them. He was certain this aggressive response would silence Muhammad (pbuh) and scare away any of his followers.

While today many Muslims are on the fence about their commitment to the religion, these early converts faced the most heinous attacks and torture but maintained their beliefs. Without a doubt, their steadfastness was of an extraordinary level and put all the weak justifications many provide today for their irreligiousity to shame.

Those early Muslims were pulled from their homes, taken out in the scorching sun, beaten and abused, and their family members were harmed before their eyes as another tool of abuse and torture. This is what Abu Jahl did to the family of Ammar; he had the soldiers take his mother Sumayyah and his father Yasir away and had them hung on a make-shift crucifix. Then they were thrown to the ground, before Ammar's eyes, to force him to look at his mother and father being abused.

This psychological torture was very traumatic and Ammar suffered deeply from the sight of the pain of his parents. He watched helplessly as the soldiers forced his mother's legs apart and put her on the rack. As they stretched her limbs further and further from her body, Abu Jahl stood above her yelling out, "Who is your Lord? Hubal, Lat, Uzza?" She would only reply that Allah (swt) was her Lord, only Allah (swt).

The torture was relentless, but she remained unbreakable in spirit. Interestingly, Umar ibn Khattab was there at the side of Abu Jahl, participating in the torture. Prior to announcing he was Muslim, he used to participate in torturing women. Abu Jahl demanded Yasir to tell him the name of his Lord, and Yasir continued to reply: Allah (swt). Abu Jahl continued to increase the pressure by unrelentingly torturing Ammar's parents before his eyes. He then went so far as to strike a spear right through his father's stomach, killing him.

He knew Ammar was under the most intense pain, yet he had no mercy for him whatsoever. He continually demanded from him, "Who is your Lord?" Ammar remained steadfast and devoted, claiming that Allah (swt) was his Lord. Abu Jahl continued to torture Ammar's mother, whipping her over and over, but still she said Allah was her Lord.

Abu Jahl wouldn't be outdone, and at this point he mocked these unflinching new Muslims claiming their Lord would be impotent against his next threat. With that blasphemous boast, he had the soldiers tie Sumayyah's battered and bruised hands to horses, and beat them to charge away. Sumayyah's cries were earth shattering, as her stomach and body were ripped open.

Today's Muslim generation in the West claim hardship in practicing their religion openly, while they have been spared such threats, traumas, and viciousness as these early Muslims endured. Even today, many Muslims are suffering similar traumas and hardships in countries such as Bahrain, Yemen, Syria, and Iraq; but those in the West have tremendous ease in comparison.

After witnessing such brutality, Ammar's spirit and determination was broken and he relented when Abu Jahl questioned him again. He said with a heavy and broken heart, that he worshipped the lord Abu Jahl worshipped. Abu Jahl puffed up with pride and emboldened by his aggression, released him, and told him to leave. Ammar was so utterly ashamed that he had said he did not believe in the one Lord.

He went repentant to the Holy Prophet's (pbuh) house, his wounds still fresh and raw. He knew that the Holy Prophet (pbuh) had advised them all to remain patient and that Jannah (Paradise) awaited them, giving them courage through the difficult and wearisome torture. But Ammar relented and uttered something which his mother hadn't even uttered. His mother died saying Allah (swt) and his father died saying Allah (swt). But Ammar had said that he did not believe in Allah (swt).

He came to the Holy Prophet (pbuh) and begged for his forgiveness and for Allah (swt) to forgive him. He told the Prophet (pbuh) how he had said something that belied what was truly in his heart due to the pressure of seeing his parents tortured so viciously, and for all that was inflicted on himself as well.

At that moment, the following verse of the Quran was revealed:

Anyone who, after accepting faith in Allah, utters Unbelief, except under compulsion, his heart remaining firm in Faith - but such as open their breast to Unbelief, on them is Wrath from Allah, and theirs will be a dreadful Penalty," (Q16:106).

This verse is the proof of *taqiyyah*, or dissimulation of faith within the Islamic belief. *Taqiyyah* is allowed in situations that are a matter of life and death, where to save one's life, the concealment of belief is permissible. While certainly the status of martyr is given to those who lose their life on account of their belief, this option is also vital for the survival of the faith in the gravest of times.

The sixth Imam, Imam Ja'far al-Sadiq (as) said, "*Taqiyyah* is my religion and the religion of my ancestors," indicating that no religion can survive the direst of pressure and threats unless there is an option of dissimulation. Another example of this dissimulation of faith was with the Companions of the Cave mentioned in the Holy Qur'an, the Ashab al-Kahf who could have never survived unless they were in *taqiyyah*.

The Holy Prophet (pbuh) himself during the first three years of his message was in *taqiyyah*, in the sense that his Companions could not come out publicly. Only after three years were they permitted to come out publicly. Likewise, Ammar was in a state of *taqiyyah*. The Holy Prophet (pbuh) assured him not to worry, that his parents were most certainly promised Jannah, and that Allah (swt) revealed a verse about him giving comfort to his pained and heavy heart.

Allah (swt) directly comforted him and assured him that He, the Divine Creator, knew what was in his heart and that he was one of the true believers.

After these years of trials, pain, and loss Ammar ibn Yasir was amongst those who accompanied the Holy Prophet (pbuh) on the *hijrah*, or migration, from Mecca to Medina. One of the first things that happened when they established themselves in Medina was the building of the Prophet's mosque. In the heat of Arabia, they would lay brick after brick, tirelessly forming the sanctuary for the believers.

Numerous *hadith* narrate that only one man would take two bricks in his hand and lay them with more fervour than anyone, and that was Ammar ibn Yasir. The Holy Prophet (pbuh) would see him tired, drenched in sweat, but perfumed by heavenly devotion. There was one individual who was avoiding getting his hands dirty, and that was Uthman ibn Affan. Ammar confronted him as he simply stood by while everyone else was actively building saying, "Those who build are not like those who turn their heads away from the dust."

Uthman was about to strike Ammar for insulting him, but the Holy Prophet (pbuh) looked at him and said, "Stop. Ammar invites people towards Paradise, and they want to take him towards Hell.

Ammar is the piece of flesh between my eyes and my nose." Ammar received that accolade from the Holy Prophet (pbuh) emphasizing how close Ammar was to him, just as the flesh between the eyes. The Holy Prophet (pbuh) chastised Uthman to never get in a situation where he would hurt him.

It was at this point that Muhammad (pbuh) gave a prophecy stating that a rebellious group calling people to hell would kill Ammar. This prophecy meant that whomever opposed and killed Ammar would indeed be confirmed publicly as evil in any future battle.

In the Battle of Badr, Ammar was protected by Allah (swt), and even later at the Battle of Khandaq, serving the community and remaining a valiant supporter of the religion. It was Ammar who led the community in digging trenches at the Battle of Khandaq. He was always committed and at the forefront of the struggle for Islam.

From the Qur'an's earliest revelations until the very last, Ammar sacrificed everything for Allah (swt) and His Prophet (pbuh), which is why no one was hurt like Ammar when he saw what was inflicted upon the son-in-law and the daughter of the Holy Prophet (pbuh). Ammar was one of the few Companions loyal to the rightful Imam, Imam Ali (as), and Fatimah al-Zahra (as). After Saqifah, six Muhajirun and six Ansar came to Imam Ali (as) claiming they were with him.

The next day, close to forty other individuals came to the home of Imam Ali (as) stating their support. The following day, Imam Ali (as) said, "If all of you are sincere in your loyalty and support for me, then tomorrow come to my door with your heads shaved." Shaving one's head signified a publicly defiant and symbolic commitment to stand and defend Imam Ali's refusal to pledge allegiance to the first caliph. If hundreds of Companions shaved their heads, it would be a symbolic show of force that a large number of Muslims were ready to obey Imam Ali. However, only Abu Dhar, Salman, Miqdad, and Ammar returned the next day with their heads shaven. Each of them bravely displayed the epitome of loyalty, steadfastness and fortitude. Ammar, like the others, successfully conveyed his desire to stand by the Imam at every turn and vowed to uphold his rights. Even when it came to the burial of Fatimah al-Zahra (as), he was one of those who carried her body to her *janazah*, or burial. He was one of those who stood alongside Imam Ali (as) in those most difficult times.

Regarding Ammar ibn Yasir's biography, there are two questions that often arise. The Battle of Yamama, which occurred after the passing of the Holy Prophet (pbuh), was one of several battles fought during the Riddah Wars that opposed a rising level of apostasy and rebellion amongst tribes that wished to invade the state of Medina. First, it is claimed that at the Battle of Yamama, Ammar went and fought alongside Abu Bakr who was acting as caliph. Because of his part in this battle, his loyalty to Imam Ali (as) is erroneously questioned.

In fact, he fought because Imam Ali (as) told him to fight the apostate and false claimant to Prophethood, Musaylimah. Imam Ali (as) informed Ammar of the intentions of this individual to destroy the religion of Islam and to overtake all the strivings and sacrifices they had made for the sake of the religion. As an interesting side note, Musaylimah was from the Christian tribe of Banu Hanifah and the region of Najd, a region from which the contemporary al-Saud family traces its descent as well.

Second, some question Ammar's role as governor of Kufa under Umar ibn Khattab. But it must be established that working under a government that differs with one's views is not unlawful, or *haram*, in the religion of Islam. One can find in the Qur'an and in the *hadith*, plenty of examples such as Prophet Yusuf (pbuh) working for a government that did not believe in God or Imam al-Ridha (as) working under Ma'mun.

While Ammar was governor of Kufa, he never gave the *khutbah*, sermon, for *salat al-jumah*, the Friday prayers. This act of defiance against the ruling caliph was a bold demonstration of Ammar's loyalty to Imam Ali (as). The *khutbah* requires a discussion of political issues and social injustices; it serves an informative, revealing, and journalistic function. Instead he only read Surah Ya Sin to demonstrate that he would not be a mouthpiece for Umar's government. In addition to this, he would remove any appointees that were not qualified for their position or were unjustly appointed by Umar. This act of justice was disliked by Umar who then removed Ammar from his position, despite the fact that the Holy Prophet (pbuh) said Ammar invites people to Paradise.

When Uthman ibn Affan came into power, Ammar saw all the Umayyads who the Holy Prophet (pbuh) had exiled coming back into the community, and worse, they were entering positions of power and prominence. The likes of Walid ibn Uqbah and Marwan ibn Hakam, and others who fought the Holy Prophet (pbuh) received privileged, yet undeserved treatment. Ammar spoke out viciously against Uthman. Sayyid Qutb in his book *Social Justice in Islam* critically outlines some of the questionable political decisions of Uthman ibn Affan.

Uthman's family came down heavy on any dissenters, for example when Abdullah ibn Masud spoke out against Uthman, Umayyads allegedly beat him until his ribs were broken. When Ammar ibn Yasir publicly dissented, he was inflicted with an injury resulting in a hernia. But this physical abuse was nothing new to Ammar ibn Yasir and certainly no deterrent for him on his lifelong quest for truth and for the sanctity of the religion of Islam.

Uthman and his family had caused a great deal of tumult that it finally ended in the caliph's murder. Ammar began to hear a rumour that Ali ibn Abi Talib (as) would be targeted for revenge. Rumours spread that Imam Ali (as) allegedly knew the killers of Uthman but would not hand them over. Aisha, one of the wives of the Prophet, accepted the accusations and she gathered an army led by Talhah, Zubayr, and others to engage in the battle known as the Battle of Jamal (the Camel).

During this period, the prophecy of Muhammad (pbuh) that rebels bound for hell would kill Ammar, once again became a report that Muslims narrated. Whichever battle that Ammar joined, people would identify the group opposing him and seeking his death to ipso facto be the unjust faction.

On the day of the Battle of Jamal, a man came out in the middle of the battlefield absolutely confused. He saw Talhah, Zubayr, and the wife of the Holy Prophet (pbuh) on one side, and he saw Ammar ibn Yasir and Ali ibn Abi Talib (as) on the other. He claimed he could not tell where the truth lay in that encounter. Only Imam Ali (as) could answer in his gracious wisdom, "Don't look at the personalities, look at the truth. First look at the truth, then judge the personalities." The wisdom of the Imam (as) seems clear to his followers, but there are over seven hundred million Muslims in the world today who do not know whether they would stand with the fourth caliph or with the Prophet's wife. Logically, if one is with the wife, then one is standing to kill the fourth caliph, and if one is with the caliph, then one is fighting the wife.

This event took place only twenty-five years after the Holy Prophet (pbuh) died. This battle was an indication that the state of the Muslims was tumultuous and precarious; therefore it is absurd to assume the Divine Guide for mankind would not have had the foresight, understanding, authority or wisdom to leave a leader behind.

The eighty-nine year old Ammar on the day of Jamal was on the front lines with Imam Ali ibn Abi Talib (as). Ammar ibn Yasir is an amazing example of devotion and strength for the Muslim youth of today who cannot enumerate accomplishments of the same calibre despite having the political freedom, strength, and resources. Imam Ali (as) was victorious at Jamal, and Ammar survived the battle to serve the Ahl al-Bayt (as) again. Imam Ali (as) had completely annihilated the opposition; Talhah and Zubayr were killed, and the remaining opposition had to beg for his forgiveness.

Now the remaining issue was the governor of Shaam, Muawiyah who was sitting in control of what today comprises Syria, Lebanon, Palestine, and Jordan. Muawiyah had not come to the aid of Uthman when he was under attack, but used the issue to his political advantage by casting about blame and dissent. In Arabic, there is a phrase that is used whenever one wants to blame someone, one will figuratively "pick up Uthman's shirt." Muawiyah did just that in his power drive for the caliphate. He used a bloodied shirt that allegedly belonged to the murdered caliph as a banner in his wars. The shirt was paraded in Damascus to appeal to the public's sympathies and sense of horror.

Muawiyah also launched a vigorous campaign against Imam Ali (as) deceiving the masses that somehow the latter was involved in the murder of Uthman. Imam Ali (as), despite diplomatic attempts to end the accusations and unrest, found no other recourse than to move against Muawiyah's forces at Siffin.

In that Battle of Siffin Ammar ibn Yasir was between ninety to ninety-three years of age, and the prophecy of the Holy Prophet (pbuh) was as yet unfulfilled, "Ammar will be killed by rebels bound for hell." The traditions say he called out:

> "Oh Allah (swt), You know if You wanted me to plunge myself into the river Furaat, I'd plunge my body in there for you. Oh Allah (swt), I know You want me to fight those people because they are a corrupt brand of people. Oh Allah (swt), if that army of Muawiyah chased me to the Hajjar (a place in Bahrain) date palms, I would still know that I am on the truth and that they are in the false. Oh soldiers of Ali (as), come join me in gaining the satisfaction of Allah (swt) and the pleasure of Ali ibn Abi Talib (as). Let us fight through this opposition army."

He spoke these brave words in remembrance of a saying of the Holy Prophet (pbuh), "Oh Ammar, if all the people go towards one way, and Ali ibn Abi Talib (as) is alone going towards another, you go on the path of Ali ibn Abi Talib (as). Oh Ammar, Ali ibn Abi Talib (as) will never guide you towards that which will destroy you. Oh Ammar, know one thing. Obedience to Ali (as) is obedience to me, and obedience to me is obedience to Allah (swt)."

Despite all of Muawiyah's and all the various factions' propaganda, bribery, and threats, all the falsehood, lies, and deception, Ammar stood by Ali ibn Abi Talib (as) his whole life.

Truly he stuck to the Imam (as) with such vigour, such tenacity that at ninety years of age he came running out onto that battlefield.

He said, "This is the day I rejoin the Holy Prophet (pbuh) and those beloved members of Aal Muhammad (as). This is the day I go back to the Holy Prophet (pbuh), go back to Fatimah al-Zahra (as)." He fought until the opposition killed him. When he was dying, he called for some water as he was fasting on that day. What they brought him instead was a drink of yogurt. He looked at it and said with a smile, "Truly the Holy Prophet (pbuh) was right when he said, 'Ammar, your last drink will be a drink of yogurt.'"

Now the well-known prophecy was fulfilled; the unjust rebels had killed Ammar. As word spread through the ranks of the opposition, the soldiers became disquieted realising they were the condmened. They were on the verge of losing their composure and their commitment to Muawiyah. But this skilled propagandist didn't miss a beat and immediately blamed Ali ibn Abi Talib (as), saying, "It was Ali who had brought Ammar to war, therefore Ali is the one who killed him."

Imam Ali (as) replied, "If that (logic) is true, then the Holy Prophet (pbuh) is the one who killed Hamzah when he brought him to war." He refuted Muawiyah's illogical and irrational accusations.

Imam Ali (as) was gravely hurt when Ammar died. He states in *Nahj al-Balaghah*, "Where is ibn Tayyihan, where is Khuzaymah ibn Thabit al-Ansari? Where is Ammar ibn Yasir?" Those companions that Imam Ali (as) had, all of them died one after another. Ammar ibn Yasir had died. Muhammad ibn Abu Bakr had died. Ibn Tayyihan had died.

Khuzaymah ibn Thabit al-Ansari had died. Salman had died. Abu Dhar had died. Miqdad had died. All of the companions of the Imam (as) were dying. Because Ammar was a backbone for Imam Ali (as), he asks, "Where is Ammar?" He could always rely on Ammar to stand with him at every hardship. Imam Ali (as) eulogized him while holding his noble head in his lap:

> Surely any Muslim who is not distressed at the murder of the son of Yasir, and is not afflicted by this grievous misfortune does not have true faith. May Allah show His mercy to Ammar the day he embraced Islam. May Allah show His mercy to Ammar the day he was killed! And may Allah show His mercy to Ammar the day he is raised to life. Certainly, I found Ammar (on such level) that three Companions of the Holy Prophet could not be named unless he was the fourth, and four of them could not be mentioned unless he was the fifth.
>
> There was none among the Holy Prophet's Companions who doubted that not only was Paradise once or twice compulsorily bestowed upon Ammar, but that he gained his claim to it (a number of times). May Paradise give enjoyment to Ammar.

Certainly, it was said (by the Holy Prophet) 'Surely, Ammar is with the truth and the truth is with Ammar. He turns wherever the truth turns. His killer will be in hell.' (*Nahj al-Balaghah*, Sermon 181)

After these finally words, Imam Ali (as) rose to perform the *janazah* and then with his own blessed hands, buried the peerless Companion and devoted Muslim, Ammar.

Works Cited

Abi Talib, Ali. *Nahjul Balagha, Peak of Eloquence: Sermons, Letters, and Sayings of Imam Ali Ibn Abu Talib* Ed. Mohammad Askari Jafery. (Elmhurst, NY: Tahrike Tarsile Quran, 1986).

Chapter 4:
Abu Dhar al-Ghaffari

Abu Dhar al-Ghaffari occupies a prominent position within the religion of Islam and is seen as one of the greatest Companions not only of the Holy Prophet (pbuh), but also of Imam Ali (as). He was an extraordinary man who fought for justice, fairness, and truth. He stood against all threats to the principles of Islam and was a man whose passion and bravery set him apart as one of the noblest Companions in Islamic history. Abu Dhar was definitively the social reformer amongst the Companions of the Holy Prophet (pbuh) and his behaviour within his society was uniquely exemplary; he was peerless in his stand against injustice.

It is well known that the very base of the religion of Islam is to stand against oppression and injustice at all times. Wherever a Muslim sees oppression or injustice in the world, he or she must stand up against it utilizing beneficial means in order to allow justice to flourish within the society. The headlines are full of stories of Muslims and non-Muslims alike who are suffering injustice and oppression.

Amongst the headlines in recent times, one observes that the incidents against the followers of the Ahl al-Bayt (as) in particular are increasing. They are massacred, imprisoned, and oppressed in Pakistan, Iraq, Bahrain, Yemen, Syria, and elsewhere for no legitimate reason whatsoever. While one's first reaction is sadness, perhaps frustration, maybe even anger, the feelings must move to positive action and start with speaking out against this injustice.

The forms of this striving, this *jihad*, can very well be with one's soul, with one's tongue, or one's wealth. One can strive to foster a healthier, more equitable, and fair society and to secure the innate rights of every human being.

Abu Dhar is a galvanizing role model, someone whose motto was to never remain silent when injustice is before you. Wherever there is *dhulm*, oppression on this Earth, it is the role of a Muslim to become Abu Dhar. Dr. Ali Shariati, in his work called, "And Once Again Abu Dhar", paints a picture of this individual and the significance of his stand. He highlights that Abu Dhar al-Ghaffari gave his life to the religion of Islam after the Holy Prophet (pbuh) passed away when certain injustices began to occur in the growing Muslim community:

> Abu Dhar was trying to develop the economic and political unity of Islam...Abu Dhar believed Islam to be the refuge of the helpless, the oppressed and the humiliated people... Abu Dhar, who had begun the struggle for the development of Islamic equality, would not be pacified and would not let the enemy be pacified either...

Abu Dhar was originally named Jundab ibn Janadah and his mother was called Ramla from the tribe of Banu Ghaffar. This tribe, an offshoot of Banu Kinanah, was an infamous tribe living between Mecca and Medina in the desolate area called Rabadhah. They were a desperate and poverty-stricken people who were feared for their highway thievery. These bandits controlled their region with threats, intimidation, and lawlessness.

Prophet Shu'ayb (pbuh), who is mentioned in the Qur'an, dealt with the same type of people and was sent by Allah (swt) to reform them. The men of this tribe were involved in this criminal way of life, terrorizing any travellers or caravans passing through their area. No one could pass without either a bribe or a fight. The young Abu Dhar, however, did not want to follow this way of life. At a young age he used to make it clear that he had no interest in participating in these acts of terror and intimidation. He preferred to live the life of a farmer or a shepherd.

The whole system of idolatry troubled him as well. While the pagan tribes of the time may have believed in the concept of one God, they created at least three hundred and sixty images and idols at the Ka'ba and other temple sites. They claimed the idols were reminders of the attributes and aspects of God, but these people were certainly astray.

His tribe of Banu Ghaffar had a particular devotion to the idol named Manat, the goddess of destiny and fate. They joined other worshippers in venerating her and offering sacrifice to her temple, which was near the seashore between Mecca and Medina. Another idol of Manat was placed in the Ka'ba as well. Worshippers would make offerings such as food items, when they sought help with their fate or outcome of some event.

Hubal was considered the main idol and the patron god of the Banu Umayyah and the pagans dedicated the Ka'ba itself to him. Manat, Lat and Uzza were considered Hubal's daughters. Ironically, while they personified God in female form, their society institutionalized misogyny. There was neither veneration nor honour of the female as evidenced by the burial of girls, the denial of basic rights, and the sale of women as property.

On one occasion, Abu Dhar's family and tribe were facing the trouble of a serious drought, and they prayed to Manat for rain, but nothing happened. They then decided to make the pilgrimage and travel to Mecca. The pilgrimage was a lucrative source of income for the power structure of Mecca, especially people like Abu Sufyan who seemed not to be a worshipper of anything but money and status.

What often happened to these pagan pilgrims is they would run out of money during their stay and then have to seek loans from the Meccan elite, thus perpetuating a constant source of profit for the Meccan elite by exploitation.

Unays, Abu Dhar's brother, encouraged him to go on this pilgrimage with the family to pray for rain and lauded the benefit that the idol Manat would bring them. Abu Dhar rejected the whole premise that some inanimate object would do anything for them at all. He refused to even consider lowering his head before anything that would neither benefit nor harm him. His brother challenged him by mentioning the whole tradition and history of this worship, and how it was ingrained in the culture.

One unfortunately sees this same tenacity within humanity today when it comes to adhering to cultural norms and traditions. Even in the school of Ahl al-Bayt (as), certain cultural traditions have taken on such a solidified and necessary form while actually being simply one method of expressing love and devotion. Whether it comes to the language of devotion, or the form of expressing grief, or the quantity of commemorations, or other issues, some have set these methods with higher priorities than they actually deserve.

The fallout for this rigid tenacity, of course, is the loss of meaning for the next generation whose life experience and needs are not reflected in the previous generation's methods and who are turned off by stubborn strictures.

Abu Dhar advised his brother Unays to move beyond the expected traditions, to free himself, and move away with him for a period of time. They travelled to their maternal uncle's house with the intention of staying until the drought was over. When the two of them went to their uncle's house as part of a spiritual striving, the rest of Banu Ghaffar became jealous and began to spread rumours about them.

They could see Abu Dhar and Unays were free thinkers, who weren't mimicking false traditions; they were striving to be pure.

These two non-conformists were upsetting the system, which the elders wouldn't tolerate. One can find the same dynamic today; someone striving to become pure and more religious threatens and intimidates the non-religious or even the anti-religious. Consequently, those striving in the way of Allah (swt) get attacked. This was the case with Abu Dhar and his brother.

The rumours started first about Unays, and what better way than to create a scandal about an illicit affair? They claimed that he had a relationship with his uncle's wife. So the rumour spread, and the uncle came to hear about it so he approached the two young men. He told them what he had heard and he also said he knew it wasn't true, but once a rumour's evil seed is planted it can create devastation.

Abu Dhar confirmed that it wasn't true, but the evil began to penetrate and the uncle began to treat the two young men differently. The discomfort between them grew and the uncle became unjust; Abu Dhar could tolerate it no longer and told his brother that they should leave. Unays resisted at first feeling that they had already been uprooted once, but his brother persisted - counselling him never to settle for an unjust situation nor allow vital principles to be abandoned.

The narrations state that Abu Dhar and Unays left their uncle and went to find the passing caravans on which to travel. A caravan was passing by en route to Mecca and Abu Dhar inquired about their journey and why they were going towards Mecca. They replied they had heard of a man who was teaching people a new way of life and a new vision of God, but only a few were privy to his message.

Abu Dhar's interest was piqued and he sent his brother forward to discover more. Unays went ahead and was the first of the brothers to meet the Holy Prophet (pbuh). When they met, Unays spoke with him and asked many questions. The Holy Prophet (pbuh) explained to him the principles of Islam, the oneness of God, and the rights of the people, but Unays and the early followers were asked not to reveal the discourse publicly.

Unays came back to Abu Dhar full of praise for the Holy Prophet (pbuh) calling him truly al-Sadiq and al-Amin, the truthful and trustworthy, describing how his face radiated with light. He was eager that his brother should meet him as well; he knew his brother would be captivated by the message because it reflected his own beliefs and actions. Abu Dhar was more than ready, but he was concerned with how he should meet the Holy Prophet (pbuh) without giving away the privacy, which Muhammad (pbuh) had asked.

Abu Dhar would not be able to go to him directly. His brother was fortunate that he accompanied the caravan and his travel companions knew how to meet up with the Holy Prophet (pbuh). His brother advised him that the best way for him to meet the Holy Prophet (pbuh) was to travel to Mecca and remain around the Ka'ba, meeting the people in a normal manner. Eventually he would be able to find the right connections and they would inform him of how to visit the Holy Prophet (pbuh).

Abu Dhar travelled to Mecca and arrived at the Ka'ba where for sometime he stood looking around, not being recognized nor recognizing anyone. He stood wondering how he could ask the people about Muhammad (pbuh); he was cautious because the mission was not public and he wondered if indeed it might even be a dangerous time.

Eventually a young man approached him asking him if he was lost or if he was looking for someone. Abu Dhar was cautious and didn't reveal his true purpose; he made casual conversation remarking on the city and the idols. The next day, the young man came back to him inquiring if he found the person he was looking for. Abu Dhar played it up that he had found him and they were enjoying their time in the city, and so on. The young man continued to ask if he was certain he didn't need any help, and Abu Dhar mentioned all was well.

Finally, on the third day, the young man came to Abu Dhar again and Abu Dhar began speaking with him inquiring of his name and wondering why this young man continued to gravitate towards him. He introduced himself as Ali (as), son of Abu Talib, and sensing that Abu Dhar really had a different purpose, asked him again if he had truly found who he was looking for. Abu Dhar was cautious, hesitating, saying he wasn't sure if this young man even knew the person he was looking for. But Ali (as) asked politely again, and Abu Dhar finally revealed that he was looking for Muhammad (pbuh), son of Abdullah. Ali (as) looked at him, one can imagine with a smile and said, "Yes I think I know him. Let's go and see him."

They went to the house of the Holy Prophet (pbuh) and Abu Dhar was greeted kindly and welcomed in. He narrated, "When I saw the face of the Holy Prophet (pbuh), I knew that I was on the right path. I knew I had come to a divinely guided man because my heart did not stop beating out of my love for this man."

He sat with him and inquired about his message and the Holy Prophet (pbuh) began to tell him about the belief in the oneness of God, Allah (swt). Immediately, the message resonated with Abu Dhar, who explained to the Holy Prophet (pbuh) that since the time he was young, he only believed that God was one and that idols had nothing to do with Him. He described how his tribe had a particular devotion to the idol by the name of Manat, the goddess of destiny but he, himself, never came near that idol.

The Holy Prophet (pbuh) went on to explain the belief in the Day of Judgment and other principles of the religion and Abu Dhar was soaking it all in, in awe of the truthful message. The Holy Prophet (pbuh) cautioned him, though, that it was not yet time to reveal this knowledge publically.

Abu Dhar understood and agreed, but one can only imagine how challenging it was to control the excitement and joy of having found such meaningful truth and to know that one was not alone in one's belief in a single God. Indeed this excitement was too much for Abu Dhar to contain, and he found his way straight to the top of the Ka'ba. There he stood announcing in a loud voice, "Oh people, my name is Jundab ibn Janadah. I am also known as a follower of the Holy Prophet (pbuh) and I swear that there is no god but God, and that Muhammad (pbuh) is the messenger of God."

Instantly, the whole of Quraysh approached him to beat him in defence of their gods and way of worship; they pulled him down and punched him incessantly. While he was on the ground, he continued calling out that he was a follower of Muhammad (pbuh). They continued attacking him, yet somehow he was able to get away and ended up back at the house of the Holy Prophet (pbuh).

The Holy Prophet (pbuh) asked him what happened to him because he was injured and looked so roughed up. Just a few moments before, Abu Dhar was agreeing to the request to keep the message private, and now he was bloody and bruised for mentioning it in public. He pleaded with the Holy Prophet (pbuh) that he only told a few as he thought he was allowed just that. The Prophet (pbuh) replied that he was permitted to speak to a few people.

No sooner had he left the house, he began proclaiming again, "Oh people, I am Jundab ibn Janadah, and I have come to tell you that there is no god but God, and that Muhammad (pbuh) is the messenger of God." Again, as soon as this happened, the pagan Meccans attacked him viciously, until Abbas, the uncle of the Holy Prophet (pbuh) came and got in the middle of the melee. He gave them a bit of news that stopped them in their tracks: he advised them that Jundab's family was the infamous Banu Ghaffar.

Everyone immediately desisted from beating him up in defence of their idols and their supposedly sacred system of belief. They departed out of fear because they knew if his father got wind of their attack, they wouldn't have a caravan, let alone goods in a caravan the next time they travelled for trading. They were more concerned with their livelihood than actually defending their beliefs.

The Holy Prophet (pbuh) spoke with Abu Dhar again, having patience with him despite Abu Dhar's fiery character, his inability to remain patient, and his rashness. Since he didn't heed the Holy Prophet's (as) request to remain patient and desist from public proclamations, he advised him to return to his tribe, the Banu Ghaffar.

Abu Dhar couldn't imagine leaving the side of the Holy Prophet (pbuh) now that he had found him amidst the amazing experience of the fledging religion in Mecca. He had finally found compatriots in Ammar, Zayd b. Haritha, and Ali (as) son of Abu Talib; he wanted to be with them.

But the Holy Prophet (pbuh) insisted that he go back to Banu Ghaffar and strive to bring them towards the religion before reaching out to a wider and unknown community. The lesson of the Holy Prophet (pbuh) was to seek to reform and support your kin and those closer to you first. Unfortunately today, Muslims hurl damaging epithets at their relatives rather than seeking to reform them.

Community members are called *munafiq* (hypocrite), *muqassir* (one who falls short of accepting the status of the Imams), *kafir* (non-believer), and so forth.

It may be that despite one's best intentions and most ardent desire to bring one's family members and children towards Islam that they turn away from religion. Ultimately, the awareness that comes from struggling to "clean one's own house" should make one more understanding and less judgmental of those in the wider community. Then when casting one's glance outward to the wider community, one will, Allah willing, be more sympathetic and less castigating.

Furthermore, this approach requires one to actively work on one's self primarily in order to do any good for anyone else, even family. This method is part of collective human wisdom; Confucius even said, "Attack the evil that is within yourself, rather than attacking the evil that is in others."

Abu Dhar followed the advice and returned to his tribe, albeit with longing for the Holy Prophet (pbuh). When he went back to Banu Ghaffar, he eventually met with their chief, Ibn Nughba. Abu Dhar spoke to him in open terms and said ibn Nughba was like a father figure to him and the chief replied in kind.

He confided in Ibn Nughba that he had joined the religion of the Holy Prophet (pbuh) that worshipped the One God. A dialogue ensued wherein Ibn Nughba was most open and interested to know if the religion made sense to Abu Dhar; he entreated him to explain it to him. So Abu Dhar began to speak with passion and fervour. He described with emotion the holistic system of the religion of Islam and how he desired to proclaim it to the whole community and explain why he didn't worship the lifeless stone called Manat.

Ibn Nughba was a man of some caution and judiciousness, and he wanted to know if there were any learned people, any intellectuals in Mecca who had joined Muhammad's (pbuh) religion. He clearly wanted to understand if people of reason, not just individuals swept up in exuberant adulation were attracted to this religion. Abu Dhar replied that indeed there were such people; Waraqah ibn Nawfal had been attracted by the religion of Islam, as well as Qays ibn Sa'd. When he heard of these two, he was satisfied and gave Abu Dhar permission to tell Banu Ghaffar.

Sometime later, Abu Dhar gathered the whole tribe of Banu Ghaffar and began to tell his story. He said that he came to them as a brother to let them know why he had become a Muslim. He began his momentous speech by saying that the reason was because of the urine of a fox. The stunned crowd looked around; they stared at him incredulously wondering if they heard him correctly. He repeated himself; it was because of the urine of a fox.

The people were waiting to hear the details of the religion as they sat perplexed. But Abu Dhar went on and told them the story of a pilgrimage to Manat that he attended with them when he was young. As was the custom, they left an offering, milk. He was the one to place it before the idol that time. When all of the tribe had returned to the caravan, he stayed behind, staring at the idol and the milk.

Then he saw a fox walking past and it started drinking the milk, and then the fox urinated all over the idol, the supposedly sacred and powerful idol. Abu Dhar asked the crowd, "If that idol could not protect itself from the urine of a fox, how would it ever protect Abu Dhar al-Ghaffari?"

Around half of the tribe was struck by this story and it made them think about the foolishness of idol worship. It began a process of reflection for them where rationally, not emotionally, they could come to a decision. From this point, they were willing to join the religion of Islam. The other half needed a different type of convincing; they wanted a prophecy. A Prophet of God, they argued, if he truly receives revelations from God, should prophesize of an event that would take place in the future.

It was an interesting balance; some were operating from the intellect and some from the spiritual and metaphysical. Abu Dhar was ready for them and he affirmed that his Prophet (pbuh) had related to him before he came back to his tribe that they were going to make this very same demand for a prophecy. The prophecy was that one day Banu Ghaffar would help the Holy Prophet (pbuh) in the land of the palm trees. At the time, the Holy Prophet (pbuh) was in Mecca, not in the land of the palm trees, which would be Medina.

The Banu Ghaffar knew he was in Mecca, the dry, rocky area and not in a land of palm trees. If and when he migrated to Medina, they proclaimed, at that time they would believe in him. They honestly thought he would never leave Mecca because it was his beloved home and they argued that no one ever leaves their home.

So this group of Banu Ghaffar delayed their decision until the Holy Prophet (pbuh) established the message in Medina. When he finally did so, the Banu Ghaffar were true to their word, and all became Muslims. However, they had not yet left the area they inhabited to join the Holy Prophet (pbuh).

It had been many years since Abu Dhar left the Holy Prophet (pbuh) in Mecca. All those years, Abu Dhar was away from the nascent Muslim community through their early and difficult struggles. While he was with Banu Ghaffar, he missed the Battle of Badr, he missed the Battle of Uhud, and he missed the Battle of Khandaq.

It wasn't until the following verse was revealed, "O ye who believe! Shall I lead you to a bargain that will save you from a grievous Penalty? - That ye believe in Allah and His Messenger, and that ye strive (your utmost) in the Cause of Allah, with your property and your persons: That will be best for you, if ye but knew!" (Q61:10-11). When Abu Dhar heard this verse, he reflected deeply on his absence and how he had not helped the Holy Prophet (pbuh) through the previous, momentous battles. From this point on he was determined to strive in the manner the Qur'an described.

The first battle in which he participated was the Battle of Khaybar. He, along with his tribe, participated in the battle; Banu Ghaffar's women were specifically the nurses at Khaybar. These women, who a few years earlier, were worshipping idols, were now nursing the wounds of the Muslim soldiers at Khaybar. Also at Khaybar, Abu Dhar observed Ali ibn Abi Talib (as) and remarked how he had grown from the helpful and astute young thirteen year-old to a strong, powerful, twenty-nine year-old warrior whose performance on the day of Khaybar was extraordinary. But at the start of that day, Ali ibn Abi Talib (as) had an eye infection that kept him from the battlefield.

So many of the other Companions thought that it was their turn to shine. Nevertheless, every single time the Holy Prophet (pbuh) gave the banner to someone, they came back without victory. Marhab, the head of the opposition was no easy man to fight, he was one of the most ferocious warriors of the Jews of Khaybar.

Sa'd ibn Abi Waqqas narrated that when the soldiers had all come back that night, the Holy Prophet (pbuh) told them that on the following morning he would give the banner to a man who loves him and Allah (swt), and that Allah (swt) and he love this man. He went on to say that when this individual goes onto the battlefield he never comes back except with victory. So everyone was wondering whom this unnamed person would be, they were wondering if it might even be one of them.

The Holy Prophet (pbuh) knew that there was only one man who would be able to defeat Marhab, so the following day he called for Ali (as) to be brought to him. When they brought him, he took some of his saliva and touched his eye. Imam Ali (as) reportedly said that he had never possessed eyesight better than on that day. Now that he could see, he was given the banner straight away. Sa'd ibn Abi Waqqas reported that Ali ibn Abi Talib (as) ran out alone towards the front and he stood there, while the rest of the soldiers were still sitting on the ground busy putting on their armour.

Marhab, the Jewish warrior, had seen in a dream the previous night that a lion would kill him, and he couldn't make sense of it. When Marhab came out to the battlefield he daringly announced his name and his lineage and his attributes in the face-to-face combat tradition. In al-Tabari it is reported that Marhab said the following lines, "Khaybar knows well that I am Marhab, whose weapon is sharp, a warrior tested. Sometimes I thrust with a spear; sometimes I strike with a sword, when lions advance in burning rage."

Then Ali ibn Abi Talib (as) came forward and met that bravado by eloquently proclaiming that he was the one whose mother had named him Haydar, the lion. Then this lion of Islam slew the undefeatable Marhab, with his sword – striking so powerful that it went through his helmet and head. The battle went on, and Ali (as) was able to advance, annihilating Marhab's brothers and more of the opposition. Ali also lifted the famous gate of Khaybar that was reportedly so heavy that multiple men were needed to replace it on its hinges.

Abu Dhar was there at the Battle of Khaybar and a witness to the incredible heroism of Ali ibn Abi Talib (as). After Khaybar came the Expedition of Tabuk, where the Muslim forces numbering up to thirty thousand moved in defence of a rumoured Byzantine threat at the edge of their frontier. The Holy Prophet (pbuh) left Ali ibn Abi Talib (as) in charge of Medina; this designation was one among many signs the Prophet (pbuh) gave indicating his future successor.

En route to the frontier, the Muslim forces experienced soaring temperatures, and a threatening drought. Abu Dhar al-Ghaffari, who was part of the forces, found himself on a camel that was excessively thirsty. This camel stopped to drink water repeatedly, thus he was lagging behind. The Holy Prophet (pbuh) and his army were moving forward at such a pace that Abu Dhar's camel could not keep up.

When they reached the area before Tabuk, some of the Companions asked the Holy Prophet (pbuh) where was the person that he always praised by saying his *taqwa*, God consciousness, was the same as Prophet Jesus (pbuh)? They mocked Abu Dhar saying that he probably had gone back home, while the rest of them were preparing for war.

No sooner had they said this, did they see Abu Dhar at a distance coming through the fiery desert and suddenly collapsing. The Holy Prophet (pbuh) ordered his men to quickly go to Abu Dhar's aid. The men found a container of water with Abu Dhar, so the Holy Prophet (pbuh) told them to give him the water. Once Abu Dhar was revived, he told the Holy Prophet (pbuh) that his camel was languishing behind as it constantly needed to relieve its thirst. He said that he himself became thirsty, but when he was about to take a sip of water, he denied himself thinking that his Prophet (pbuh) may be thirsty.

He couldn't bring himself to drink knowing that the Holy Prophet (as) may have been in need and suffering. He was happy with what he did even though he nearly died because of it. Because of his peerless devotion and piety that separated him from others, the Holy Prophet (pbuh) at that moment said, "Lonely was Abu Dhar in this world. Lonely when he was alive. Lonely when he dies. Lonely when he is resurrected."

Abu Dhar was one of the lonely few who were willing to openly stand with Imam Ali (as) after Saqifa. He didn't have any doubt about what the Prophet (as) meant on the Day of Ghadir when he said, "For whomsoever I am his Leader (*mawla*), Ali (as) is his Leader (*mawla*)."

There are narrations that on the day of Ghadir, after his appointment of Ali as successor, the Holy Prophet (pbuh) asked Abu Dhar exclusively to always stand and confirm his appointment. This is likely why you find Abu Dhar with Salman, Miqdad, and Ammar standing by Imam Ali (as) after Saqifa.

They were the loyal, uncompromising supporters who came with their shaved heads. They were the select few that were permitted to carry the Lady of Light, Fatima Zahra (as) to her final resting place. In fact, Abu Dhar al-Ghaffari was actually the one who was holding the front of Fatima Zahra's (as) *janazah*, and he is the one that narrated, "I saw Imam Hasan (as) and Imam Husayn (as) over their mother's body crying."

He said, "Especially when I saw the young Husayn (as) crying that much, I bear witness I saw Ali (as) speaking to Jibreel, the archangel. Jibreel was telling him 'Remove Husayn (as) from the chest of his mother, for the angels cannot bear to see Imam Husayn (as) crying on the chest of his mother'." That is why the famous poet says, "If the angels couldn't bear to see Imam Husayn (as) on the chest of his mother, then how did they bear to see Shimr sitting on his chest?"

Abu Dhar al-Ghaffari was one of the privileged few at the janazah of Fatima Zahra (as) and continued to remain amongst the loyal ones of the Ahl al-Bayt (as). The narrations state that in the time of the first and second caliph, he was quiet and did not make any vocal opposition.

While Ammar ibn Yasir did take a position as the governor of Kufa on the command of Imam Ali (as), Abu Dhar al-Ghaffari did not. He remained patient and silent during the reigns of the first and second caliphs. However, when the third caliph came in, nobody was as outspoken against Uthman ibn Affan as Abu Dhar al-Ghaffari.

He witnessed the Umayyads unjustly dividing and consuming the *bayt al-maal*, the treasury of the Muslims. This was akin to the siphoning away of the very meaning and purpose of the religion: to bring equity and social justice to humanity. The likes of Marwan ibn Hakam, who the Holy Prophet (pbuh) expelled from the Islamic state, received five hundred thousand *dinar*. Marwan ibn Hakam was not even brought back during the caliphate of Abu Bakr nor Umar, but Uthman brought him back and gave this man great access to public funds.

Uthman also gave Haarith ibn Hakim three hundred thousand *dinars* and Zayd ibn Thabit one hundred thousand *dinars* from the *khums* (a tax of one-fifth) of Africa. One after another, the treasury of the people was being unjustly depleted to pad the pockets of the former elite from the Time of Ignorance.

The aristocrats who had lost their position, prestige, and privilege with the arrival of the message for humanity, Islam, were beginning to take hold of the chains of power and control, one after another.

Abu Dhar saw this injustice and he was vocal in questioning Uthman, but Uthman would deny any wrongdoing claiming his right to authority and decision-making. Abu Dhar was incensed that Uthman was giving the people's money to characters that did not deserve it at all. His anger was for the sake of Allah (swt) not for any personal reason, and Imam Ali (as) would speak of this on a very sorrowful day.

Even today the state of poor Muslim countries indicates the richest and most powerful people at the top are not distributing wealth and serving its people according to the Holy Prophet's (pbuh) guidelines. Even further, when one observes that there are poor people among the followers and descendants of the Ahl al-Bayt (as), the *khums* is not being distributed properly.

Abu Dhar saw this very same misuse of *khums*. He was incessantly vocal against Uthman, to the point where he was becoming a major threat to his authority. Uthman then exiled him to Shaam (Damascus), where even greater extravagance and abuse of power occurred under the banner of Islam.

In Shaam, Muawiyah was governor and the excess was extraordinary. The city was just dripping in Byzantine-influenced opulence. There, Abu Dhar saw the green palace, the Khidrah, that Muawiya built and criticized it as extravagant. Ironically, while today the shrines of the Ahl al-Bayt (as) and their devoted followers, like Hujr ibn Adi, are bombed and ripped apart with the calls of *Allahu Akbar*, God is the Greatest, the Umayyad mosques and palaces are left in pristine condition.

Abu Dhar could not rectify in his mind and heart that the supposed Muslim caretaker of Shaam, Muawiyah, had a grand palace while there were poor people in the streets. While he and his father claimed to be sincere converts to Islam, in reality they were war criminals set free upon the Conquest of Mecca. Even Zaynab (as) told Yazid in his palace, "Oh you whose father was freed by my grandfather (pbuh)."

Abu Dhar took a stand by publicly calling to the good, and forbidding evil. Every morning he stood outside Muawiyah's palace reciting:

O ye who believe! There are indeed many among the
priests and anchorites, who in Falsehood devour the
substance of men and hinder (them) from the way of
Allah. And there are those who bury gold and silver
and spend it not in the way of Allah: announce unto
them a most grievous penalty. (Q9:34)

He continued without ceasing and would not let Muawiyah rest.
Muawiyah would send Amr ibn al-Aas to Abu Dhar with placations
and gifts, thinking money would somehow stop this self-less and
devoted servant of the Holy Prophet (pbuh). It appears he also sent
Abu Darda with the same money trying in desperation to silence Abu
Dhar. He would refuse to take any money continuously reminding
them that the Holy Prophet (pbuh) taught his followers to speak out
against injustice.

He even told Muawiyah that he was an unjust man even if his
palace was built from his own money, since it was still an extravagant
and excessive indulgence, improper for a representative of the Holy
Prophet's (pbuh) mission. If it was from the Muslim's money, then
it was certainly illegal and treason against the Muslim community.
Furthermore, he was continually bringing the residents of Shaam
towards the love of the Holy Household (as) and those believers, still
found today in Syria, are because of this truth-speaker, Abu Dhar. He
continued his protest until Muawiyah could no longer risk such
dissent in his region and the rising discontent with the Caliph
Uthman.

Muawiyah had Abu Dhar exiled to Jabal Amel, Lebanon. Today many of the followers of the Ahl al-Bayt (as) come from Jabal Amel, and it is one of the greatest places for scholarship in the school of Ahl al-Bayt (as) as well. Abu Dhar al-Ghaffari had been the man who stood like a pillar in Jabal Amel guiding people towards the love of the Holy Household (as).

Muawiyah heard that in Jabal Amel, the people were becoming followers of Ahl al-Bayt (as) because of this continually vocal Abu Dhar. He ordered soldiers to remove Abu Dhar from Jabal Amel and take him back to Uthman, but on a horse without a saddle. Such a long ride would be extremely painful. He rode all the way to Uthman ibn Affan in Medina on a horse without a saddle, and some narrations say without even being allowed to stop. It is a wonder that in other schools of Islam, individuals who order such treatment toward their fellow Muslims, and the killing and torture of others are still considered worthy of going to Jannah.

Once back in Medina, Abu Dhar would not leave Uthman ibn Affan alone either, continuing his campaign for justice and the protection of the Islamic mission. He would criticize him for his policies as caliph; for giving positions of authority back to his undeserving family members, and fleecing the treasury of the Muslims. Uthman made a decision to end his vociferous dissent by exiling him to the region of his birth, the desolate and poor area of Rabadhah near Medina.

Uthman deputised Marwan ibn Hakam to eject him from the city, even though both Marwan and his father Hakam were cursed and exiled by the Prophet. He also ordered that no one was allowed to speak to him nor see him off, but a significant few disregarded this order – specifically Imam Ali (as), Imam Hasan (as), Imam Husayn (as), Aqil ibn Abi Talib, Abdullah ibn Ja`far and Ammar ibn Yasir. Imam Ali (as) spoke to Abu Dhar assuring him of the unseen truth:

> O Abu Dhar! You showed anger in the name of Allah therefore have hope in Him for whom you became angry. The people were afraid of you in the matter of their (pleasure of this) world while you feared them for your faith. Then leave to them that for which they are afraid of you and get away from them taking away what you fear them about. How needy are they for what you dissuade them from and how heedless are you towards what they are denying you. You will shortly know who is the gainer tomorrow (on the Day of Judgment) and who is more enviable. Even if these skies and earth were closed to some individual and he feared Allah, then Allah would open them for him. Only rightfulness should attract you while wrongfulness should detract you. If you had accepted their worldly attractions they would have loved you and if you had shared in it they would have given you asylum. (*Nahj al-Balaghah*, Sermon 129)

He was cruelly and inhumanely given a protracted death sentence and exiled to starve in Rabadhah along with his devoted wife, daughter, and son. Imam Ali (as) was unable to fight the majority of Muslims who acquiesced silently to this crime and, and could not protect Abu Dhar; the religion and young community were in a precarious position.

But Abu Dhar did not seek anything other than the pleasure of Allah (swt) and he conveyed to Imam Ali (as) that it was his honour to be in a position where he could sacrifice in order to speak for his Imam's (as) right and the truth.

It is reported that Ammar ibn Yasir could not stop crying when Abu Dhar was exiled; he was so overcome. He was on the verge of falling unconscious because he could not believe that Abu Dhar would be left in a desert alone with no supplies, no food, no resources and no one to help him.

Abu Dhar al-Ghaffari, about whom the Holy Prophet (pbuh) said, "Nothing but truth comes out of his mouth," Abu Dhar al-Ghaffari, about whom the Holy Prophet (pbuh) said, "The heavens and the earth have never seen a man walk on the grass like Abu Dhar," Abu Dhar al-Ghaffari, about whom the Holy Prophet (pbuh) said, "His *taqwa* is the same as Jesus (pbuh), son of Mary (as)," was left alone in a desert. He was left alone to die alone.

On the first day of the exile, the son and wife had nothing to eat except some wild plants, and unbeknownst to them they were poisonous - leading to their painful and sorrowful death. His daughter distraught over witnessing her mother and brother's death asked her father, if they were on the *haqq*, the truth? He confirmed indeed they were for there would be no other reason why they would find themselves in such a situation. The caliph and his governor couldn't outright kill this beloved Companion of the Holy Prophet (pbuh) so they removed him from the people's sight and hearing to silence him and his calls for justice.

He assured her that though not apparent yet, the truth of all they endured and lost would be manifest in the Hereafter, and the generous reward of their Lord would come, just as Imam Ali (as) stated. One can imagine him describing to his devoted daughter that the evildoers of the world want to destroy truth, want to wipe it off the face of the earth; but they are the ones that do not believe in the Day of Reckoning, "Lo! thy Lord is ever watchful," (Qur'an, 89.14).

Her father reassured her that when he was to die that someone would come as promised by Imam Ali (as) to perform his burial and lead the prayers. The narrations state that Malik al-Ashtar came and found Abu Dhar's daughter sitting by the road alongside the body of her noble father. He was the one sent by Imam Ali (as) to lead the *janazah*, burial rites, of Abu Dhar. When Malik finished the *janazah* the tears were flowing from his eyes as he reflected on what the powers in the world had done to a person like Abu Dhar, a person who left everything to help the religion of Islam, who brought his tribe and countless other people towards Islam, and then ended up exiled and dying in a harsh and desolate land.

Meanwhile those treacherous ones who were involved in his death by exile sat in palaces and grand homes. In the beginning of this religion, Muawiyah ibn Abu Sufyan was the biggest enemy of the religion, and Abu Dhar was the biggest supporter; Malik al-Ashtar cried because of this tragic turn of events.

Imam Ali (as), too, was devastated when Abu Dhar died. His tears flowed for this man who he had found beside the Ka'ba searching eagerly for the Holy Prophet (pbuh) so many years before. His tears flowed for the man who proclaimed truth and lived the commands of Islam and suffered so many abuses doing so.

His tears flowed for the one who came with a shaven head to aid him, the rightful successor to the Holy Prophet (pbuh). His tears flowed for the one who brought so many towards the love of the Ahl al-Bayt (as). His tears flowed for the man who heeded all his advice about living in this transient world, "Be conscious of Allah (swt), and be steadfast in your religion. Do not yearn for this world. Nor should you be seduced by it. Do not resent anything that you have missed in it. Always proclaim the truth. Oppose the oppressor. Support the oppressed."

Truly Abu Dhar al-Ghaffari embodied the guidance of the religion of Islam and the words of the blessed Imam Ali (as). The believers will await the day when he will be resurrected alone to receive his reward for being the indefatigable caller to justice.

Works Cited

Abi Talib, Ali. *Nahjul Balagha, Peak of Eloquence: Sermons, Letters, and Sayings of Imam Ali Ibn Abu Talib* Ed. Mohammad Askari Jafery. (Elmhurst, NY: Tahrike Tarsile Quran, 1986).

Al-Kalbi, Hisham ibn *The Book of Idols, Being a Translation from the Arabic of the Kitab al-Asnam.* Trans. Nabih Amin Faris. (Princeton: Princeton University Press, 1952).

al-Tabari. *The History of al-Tabari: The Victory of Islam.* (Albany: State University Of New York, 1997).

Confucius. *The Analects.* Trans. D. C. Lau. (New York: Penguin Books, 1979).

Shariati, Ali. *And Once Again Abu Dhar. The cultural heritage series of the Islamic revolution.* (Tehran: Abu Dhar Foundation, 1985).

DR. SAYED AMMAR NAKSHAWANI

Chapter 5:

Muhammad ibn Abu Bakr

Muhammad ibn Abu Bakr occupies a prominent position in Islamic history and is revered as one of the greatest companions of Imam Ali ibn Abi Talib (as). He is arguably the most pivotal companion of the Ahl al-Bayt (as) in early Islam in the sense that from every angle he has a bearing on the development of Islamic history and Islamic theology. If you want to refer to Islamic legal theory, you can refer to Muhammad ibn Abu Bakr. If you want to refer to Islamic ethics, you can refer to Muhammad ibn Abu Bakr. If you want to refer to Islamic history, you can refer to Muhammad ibn Abu Bakr. But today's Muslim community is unaware of this significant role that he played.

When one examines his biography, one finds that he is an important figure for a number of connections, be it because of his father, be it because of his step-father, be it because of his sister, the wife of the Prophet, or his stands in different areas in his life.

When the identity of his father is mentioned as Abu Bakr, there is an immediate assumption that he would naturally have sided with his father in Islamic political theory. In fact, one may find that Muhammad ibn Abu Bakr, until today, is the most controversial companion of Ali ibn Abi Talib (as) and the schools of Islam reflect this attitude in their differing opinions about his position. But on a number of levels he is relatable, most specifically to today's Muslim youth. In addition, many can find in him a role model for dealing with conflict within a family structure.

Muhammad ibn Abu Bakr was the son of the person recognized by many Muslims as the first caliph in Islamic history. Abu Bakr occupies a prominent position in many schools in Islam that revere as the first caliph and attribute to him other merits and distinctions as well. When you look at early Islamic history, Abu Bakr is considered one of the earliest converts to the religion of Islam.

Many of the works of *sirah* (biography) of the Holy Prophet (pbuh), indicate that Abu Bakr was the forty-first convert to the religion of Islam, although the more widespread claim from some schools in Islam is that Abu Bakr was the first or the second. He is also noted as the man sent by the Prophet to ransom and free Bilal ibn Rabah al-Habashi from the extreme torture he was receiving at the hands of Umayyah.

Abu Bakr accompanied the Holy Prophet (pbuh) on the night of Hijrah while Imam Ali (as) was sleeping on the bed of the Holy Prophet (pbuh) and was, according to other schools in Islam, the man who was with the Holy Prophet (pbuh) in the cave. In the Qur'an, Allah (swt) talks of this incident:

> If ye help not (your leader), (it is no matter): for Allah
> did indeed help him, when the Unbelievers drove him
> out: he had no more than one companion; they two
> were in the cave, and he said to his companion, "Have

no fear, for Allah is with us": then Allah sent down His peace upon him, and strengthened him with forces which ye saw not, and humbled to the depths the word of the Unbelievers. But the word of Allah is exalted to the heights: for Allah is Exalted in might, Wise. (Q9:40)

Finally, he is revered because of his status as the father-in-law of the Holy Prophet (pbuh) through his daughter Aisha, who was a later wife of the Holy Prophet (pbuh).

The school of Ahl al-Bayt (as) is often criticized for not recognizing these noteworthy historical incidents as reasons for revering Abu Bakr. The difference is that in the school of Ahl al-Bayt (as), his full biography until the end of his life is examined and compared to the message and teachings of the Holy Prophet (pbuh). Furthermore, how he adhered to these edicts after the Holy Prophet's (pbuh) death is examined and evaluated. In particular, his treatment of the family of the Holy Prophet (pbuh) after his demise is noteworthy and significant.

But even during the lifetime of the Holy Prophet (pbuh), we observe him disobeying the commands of the Holy Prophet (pbuh) whom the Qur'an says has a greater right over the believers than they have over themselves[1]. In *Islam: Faith, Practice & History* by Sayyid

---

[1] It is interesting to note that several of the Qur'an translations for this verse (Pickthall, Shakir, and Muhsin Khan) use the English word "close" for the Arabic word "awla". Awla means authority or right, not proximity or connection, thus the translation from these sources seems to be circumventing the establishment of the Prophet's authority here.

Muhammad Rizvi, the author emphasizes that the Holy Prophet's (pbuh) commands are binding:

> Moreover, the Prophet had the right to make laws for the people, and his orders took precedence over everyone else's idea or opinion, and his commands on social and other matters had to be carried out. Allah says, *"The Prophet has a greater authority over the believers than they themselves have"* (Q33:6). He also says, *"When Allah and His messenger have decreed a matter, it is not for any believing man or woman to have a choice in the matter"* (Q33:36). (Lesson 16)

The first point against Abu Bakr that the school of Ahl al-Bayt (as) discusses is his disobedience to the Holy Prophet's (pbuh) command. The Holy Prophet (pbuh) asked Abu Bakr to have the army come under the leadership of Usama, but he refused because he objected to being under the leadership of an eighteen-year-old.

The Holy Prophet (pbuh) made a statement on that day, "*La'nah* goes on those who do not join the army of Usama." This strong statement of the Holy Prophet (pbuh) means that he asked for Allah (swt) to withdraw his mercy from those who disobeyed and did not join the army of Usama. In Sunni sources Abu Bakr, amongst others, did not join the army of Usama. Furthermore, they claim Abu Bakr was given a prestigious status for leading the final *salah*, or prayer, before the demise of the Holy Prophet (pbuh) and this was indicative of his worthiness and prominence to become the successor.

However, that final prayer he led was taking place at the time he was meant to be with the army under the leadership of Usama. Clearly an event that transpired during the time of a direct disobedience to the Holy Prophet (pbuh) cannot logically have a meritorious status.

In addition, The Holy Prophet (pbuh) had announced Imam Ali (as) as his successor and the first caliph at least twice in his lifetime. First, on the day that the Holy Prophet (pbuh) announced his prophethood to his family as ordained by Allah (swt) and second, towards the end of his life - on the day of Ghadir.

Even though Abu Bakr and Umar were present at the Ghadir announcement, they formed an exclusive election that took place at the Saqifah (portico) of Bani Sa'ida, immediately after the Holy Prophet's (pbuh) death. There, Umar pledged allegiance to Abu Bakr, even though they both knew the position of Ali ibn Abi Talib (as).

Near the end of his life, Abu Bakr admitted that what happened at Saqifah was an error, but claimed Allah (swt) protected them from any evil consequences. After the death of the Holy Prophet (pbuh), Abu Bakr denied Fatimah al-Zahra (as) the land of Fadak that had been given to her by the Holy Prophet (pbuh) four years before his death, claiming that prophets do not leave behind inheritance.

Fatimah al-Zahra (as) herself spoke out against Abu Bakr's edict and recited all the verses relating to prophets that left behind inheritance. For example, Sulayman inherited from Dawud and Yahya from Zakariya. But more importantly, the piece of land wasn't an inheritance because it had been given to her prior to his death. According to many narrations, seeing Fatimah al-Zahra (as) so outspoken, Abu Bakr instigated Umar ibn Khattab to confront Fatimah al-Zahra (as) and this led to the public raid of her home.

It is important to establish that all Muslims are unanimous in the prohibition and disapproval of anyone who angers the family of the Holy Prophet (pbuh). If this is an unequivocal fact, it must also be recognized that Fatimah al-Zahra (as) was angered by Abu Bakr's actions so much so that she did not want him at her funeral. This narration is within the most famous books of the Sunni school of thought.

In addition, Fatimah al-Zahra's (as) anger with someone is equivalent to the anger of the Holy Prophet (pbuh) and Allah (swt) based on the well-known tradition of the Holy Prophet (pbuh), "Fatimah (as) is a part of me. Whoever angers her, angers me." It is due to these events that Abu Bakr's status and prominence is not revered in the school of the Ahl al-Bayt (as), but at the same time this point of view doesn't warrant inflammatory and dangerous rhetoric that causes bloodshed and extreme discord. It must be an academic and intellectual discussion that seeks out truth and accuracy, not emotionality and reactions.

Abu Bakr originally was married to a lady named Qutayla who did not become a Muslim when he joined the religion and remained a polytheist. Therefore he had to remarry. He married a lady by the name of Umm Rumaan who did convert and in addition he married the lady who would give birth to their son – Muhammad ibn Abu Bakr. Muhammad's mother, in Islamic history, and in the school of Ahl al-Bayt (as), is regarded as one of the greatest woman in Islamic history after the four women of Paradise.

Sheikh Saduq narrates that even the Imams of Ahl al-Bayt (as) said, "Jannah, heaven, awaits Muhammad ibn Abu Bakr's mother, Asma bint Umays, after Maryam (as), Khadijah (as), Fatimah (as) and Asiya (as) because of her courage and the stand she took in her life." There is a *hadith* that says, "Jannah yearns for four women. Three of those women are from the Umays family." Asma, Muhammad's mother, was the daughter of Umays ibn Ma'ad who was a prominent man of Arabia and her mother was Hind bint Awf.

Her sisters were all married to noble and distinguished men. Her eldest sister, Salma bint Umays, was married to Hamzah ibn Abdul Muttalib, the uncle of the Holy Prophet (pbuh). Asma's other sister, her half sister, Maymuna, was married to the Holy Prophet (pbuh).

Asma was originally married to Ja'far ibn Abu Talib, the brother of Imam Ali (as) and made many significant sacrifices for the sake of the religion. Her husband, Ja'far al-Tayyar asked her to go to Africa to spread the religion of Islam. It was a major effort to travel such distances, to leave all the familiarity and comfort of home and family to go to an unknown place and be amongst foreign people.

She agreed readily and travelled with her husband to what we know today as modern day Ethiopia. They established themselves there and began a family; their first son and first Muslim to be born in Africa was the future husband of Sayedah Zaynab (as), Abdullah ibn Ja'far. They remained there until the seventh year after Hijrah, or migration, when she formally returned to Medina.

There are *hadiths* which also state that she was present at a number of significant events in the family of the Ahl al-Bayt (as) back in Medina, such as at the wedding of Fatimah (as), the birth of Imam Hasan (as) in the second year after Hijrah, as well as at the wedding of Aisha to the Prophet (pbuh). According to Allamah Majlisi in Volume Ten of "Bihar al-Anwar" he supports the idea that she travelled between the two cities via the port cities, such as Jeddah. She would return back to Medina to support and serve Aal Muhammad (as).

Regarding Asma's descendants, some people are curious about the following *hadith* attributed to Imam Ja'far al-Sadiq (as) and often used in debates between the schools of thought, "I am blessed that I will receive the *shafa'ah* of Abu Bakr on the Day of Judgment, because he is my great grandfather."

Genealogically, Imam al-Sadiq's (as) mother, Umm Farwah, wife of Imam al-Baqir (as), was the daughter of Qasim, son of Muhammad, son of Abu Bakr. This familial connection is a point that is always raised in debates in an effort to give legitimacy to Abu Bakr by saying Muhammad ibn Abu Bakr's grand-daughter, Umm Farwah, was the wife of Imam al-Baqir (as).

First, this *hadith* is not found in any of the Imami books. Second, the *isnad* (chain of narrators) of the *hadith* even according to the evaluation of Sunni scholars state that the narrators are known for their hatred towards Imam Ali ibn Abi Talib (as). Third, Imam al-Sadiq (as), would not be in need of the *shafa'ah* of anyone else when he has the *shafa'ah* of his grandfather, the Holy Prophet (pbuh).

Finally, Imam al-Sadiq (as) is a *shafi*, or granted with the gift of intercession, because according to all of the Islamic schools, a person who is an *alim*, or learned scholar, has *shafa'ah*, and a person who is a *shahid*, or martyr, has *shafa'ah*. Based on all the above points, therefore, this *hadith* is not tenable. There is one more point as well, although less known and related to detailed, historical analysis. Umm Farwah's father Qasim ibn Muhammad was Qasim ibn Muhammad ibn Abu Samara not ibn Abu Bakr. Sayed Ja'far Murtadha al-Amali, a great Lebanese scholar has a thorough work analysing this whole tradition in depth.

The Holy Prophet (pbuh) had high regard for Asma and was once asked by Umar if he or Asma was closer to the Holy Prophet (pbuh), to which he replied that Asma bint Umays was closer. Umar was surprised and asked why that was so, and the Holy Prophet (pbuh) told him that he had done one *hijrah*, from Mecca to Medina whereas Asma went from Mecca to Africa, then Africa back to Medina.

So when Asma's husband Ja'far al-Tayyar was killed in the Battle of Mu' ta, the Holy Prophet (pbuh) himself came to pay his respects to this esteemed lady. He started rubbing the heads of Ja'far's children and Asma realised what this tender gesture meant. She asked the Holy Prophet (pbuh) if her children had become orphans.

He affirmed that in fact they had, but he gave her the most beautiful message assuring her that Allah (swt) had bestowed upon her courageous and pious husband a most fitting gift; Allah (swt) had replaced his hands lost in battle with wings with which he would fly in Jannah, or Paradise. Asma was deeply comforted by these words from the Holy Prophet (pbuh), and turned her attention to her three children.

Remarriage would be the only way for her to support the children. A proposal came forth from Abu Bakr, who at this point, was in good standing as a Companion of the Holy Prophet (pbuh). She accepted the proposal and nine months later they had a son whom they named Muhammad.

It is fascinating to note that Muhammad ibn Abu Bakr was the first Muslim to be born during Hajj, and even more interesting was that the birth took place at the *miqat,* or starting point for Hajj, of Masjid Shajarah. This occasion brought about a lengthy discussion in the books of Islamic law, where one can find whole sections called "The Birth of Muhammad ibn Abu Bakr" regarding the discussion of whether a woman can perform Hajj while pregnant and other related questions regarding women's issues and Hajj, and specifically if she can continue from the *miqat* of Masjid Shajarah after giving birth.

Asma asked the Holy Prophet (pbuh) to join him on his Hajj while she was pregnant and he agreed. At Masjid Shajarah Asma gave birth, and the Holy Prophet (pbuh) granted her permission to perform her *ghusl*, the full ablution, wear her *ihram*, garments for Hajj, and from there continue with the Hajj. There were stipulations when it came time for the *tawaf*, circumambulation, and regarding *ghusl*.

A few months after this blessed Hajj, the Holy Prophet (pbuh) passed away and Asma began to notice that her husband and his companions were shifting their loyalties and preparing to launch an attack on the lady she admired the most. This was an incredible predicament for her in determining where here loyalties lay. She knew the noble and beloved daughter of the Holy Prophet (pbuh) Fatimah al-Zahra (as) and Ali ibn Abi Talib (as) as the most devoted servants of the religion and beloved and honoured family of the Holy Prophet (pbuh).

She observed the preparations for the raid on Fatimah al-Zahra's (as) house and the harm done to the beloved daughter of the Holy Prophet (pbuh). For sure, this loyal supporter of the religion, Asma, was caught in the middle of significant figures, on the one hand, she was a loyal devotee of the Holy Prophet (pbuh) and the religion, and on the other she is related to Abu Bakr and Aisha. Asma bint Umays drew a line in the sand, husband or no husband, when it came to her principles: Allah (swt) and Ahl al-Bayt (as) came first.

When Fatimah al-Zahra (as) was suffering from the attack on her home and was in her final days, Aisha, the stepdaughter of Asma, came to visit her. Asma would not allow her to enter the house. Aisha was incensed and offended that her status wasn't respected and that she was told to leave.

In a number of Sunni references, including *History of Ibn al-Athir* and *Lisan al-Arab*, Aisha agreed with her father and advised him not to recognize any inheritance of the Prophet (pbuh). By defending her father, Abu Bakr, in the confiscation of the property of Fatimah al-Zahra (as), Asma wouldn't even hear Aisha's demands.

Asma bint Umays did all she could to tend to the affairs of Fatimah al-Zahra (as), such as her *ghusl*, even though it was against Abu Bakr's wishes. She knew she would have to answer before Allah (swt) and her duty was to Him above anyone else. She took Muhammad, her infant son, with her to the *ghusl* of Fatimah al-Zahra (as). She is the one who prepared the cover of Fatimah al-Zahra's (as) body according to the specific wishes of Fatimah al-Zahra (as) that her body shape not show.

Fatimah al-Zahra (as), even when she was dying, was concerned about her hijab. When the *ghusl* was completed, Asma took some bamboo sticks to create a makeshift coffin around the body of Fatimah al-Zahra. She also covered the body with the *kaffan*, burial cloth, keeping her figure private. She is the one who narrates about

Imam Ali (as) washing the body of Fatimah al-Zahra (as) and how he began to weep. It is clear from the nature of Asma's reports, she was an intimate friend of the Family of the Prophet (pbuh).

Asma's decision to stand by the Ahl al-Bayt (as) and maintain her principles caused a great deal of friction between her and her husband Abu Bakr. He lived for two years after the death of the Prophet and then he died. From the age of two, Muhammad ibn Abu Bakr was brought up by Ali ibn Abi Talib (as), and Asma married Imam Ali (as) at this point as well.

Imam Ali (as) used to describe Muhammad ibn Abu Bakr as his son from the line of Abu Bakr, demonstrating the close connection and affinity they had for each other. From the time of his toddler years up into his youth Muhammad ibn Abu Bakr would follow Ali ibn Abi Talib (as) everywhere. Imam Hasan (as) and Imam Husayn (as) were ten and nine years old respectively when he came to live with them, and they used to treat Muhammad ibn Abu Bakr as their younger brother.

This young Muhammad grew up as well under the caliphate of Umar and Uthman, and while these two never had any antipathy towards him, they definitely kept a pulse on him as the son of Abu Bakr. They hoped that he would continue the legacy of his father.

On the contrary, he vocally and emphatically disassociated from his father and in many *hadiths* on this topic he said, "I disassociate completely from anything to do with my father of birth. My spiritual father is Imam Ali (as). Everything I learn in this world is due to Ali ibn Abi Talib (as), in the way he looked after my mother and the way he brings discipline into the religion of Islam." He was only about eighteen or nineteen years of age when he began to see the oppression of the third caliph Uthman with respect to his government appointees. In fact, these are the events that led to the Battle of Jamal, where a confrontation between brother and sister is also part of the story.

The whole predicament began with Uthman bringing many Umayyads back into positions of power, like Marwan ibn Hakam, exiled by the Holy Prophet (pbuh), Abdullah ibn Abi Sarh, exiled by the Holy Prophet (pbuh), and Walid ibn Uqbah, exiled by the Holy Prophet (pbuh) and criticized in the Qur'an as an outright *fasiq*, or a violater of Islamic law.

Uthman brought ibn Abi Sarh back and always sought to protect him even when the Prophet had ordered his execution. The people of Egypt were disgruntled at a blatant example of nepotism when Abdullah ibn Abi Sarh, Uthman's foster brother-in-law, was appointed governor of Egypt. They believed someone who had outright apostatized, denied Prophethood and Divine revelation, was not suitable to represent the successor to the Prophet (pbuh). Amongst the people in Egypt who spoke out against Abdullah ibn Abi Sarh, was Muhammad ibn Hudhayfah who reminded the people that this man used to openly fight the Holy Prophet (pbuh) and even alter words when transcribing the Qur'an.

Now this Abdullah ibn Abi Sarh, someone who made a mockery of the religion, in toying about with it in the Prophet's lifetime (pbuh), had somehow been put in the position of representing it.

What a dire situation where other more qualified candidates were ignored and pushed aside. For example there were excellent and impeccable alternatives such as Abdullah ibn Masud, Abu Dhar al-Ghaffari, Salman al-Muhammadi, Miqdad ibn al-Aswad, and Jabir ibn Abdullah al-Ansari. Muhammad ibn Hudhayfah continued to protest against Abdullah ibn Abi Sarh and Uthman tried to put a stop to his campaign through bribery.

That tactic served to cause further problems and only backfired. When Uthman discovered that ibn Hudhayfah had dissented, he wrote him a letter accompanied with extravagant clothing and thirty thousand *dinar* to buy his silence and continue protecting Abdullah ibn Abi Sarh.

The people of Egypt finally chased out Abdullah ibn Abi Sarh, and Muhammad ibn Abu Bakr became associated with the movement of Muhammad ibn Hudhayfah. Eventually the movement against Uthman grew and the people of Medina began to demand justice.

Within Sunni *hadiths* it is claimed that Muhammad ibn Abu Bakr killed Uthman ibn Affan; for example one *hadith* says, "Muhammad ibn Abu Bakr held the beard of Uthman and said to him, you the oppressor, I am the one who is going to end your life."

From the school of Ahl al-Bayt (as) these *hadiths* are not considered valid for a number of reasons.

First, Muhammad ibn Abu Bakr never acted politically without the command of Imam Ali (as) and Imam Ali (as) did not want the aggrieved people to kill Uthman. Imam Ali (as) actually went to Uthman to counsel him to be cautious about whom he was allowing to influence him, such as Marwan ibn Hakam. Number two, Imam Ali (as) put Imam Hasan (as) and Imam Husayn (as) outside the door of Uthman to defend him. Imam Ali (as) went to protect Uthman and sought to advise Uthman.

A large group put Uthman ibn Affan under siege before he was finally killed. Leading Companions, including Aisha, Talhah, Zubayr and Abdul Rahman b. Udays, encouraged protest against Uthman's policies. Ibn Udays was a prominent organizer of the siege against Uthman. His conduct testifies to the difficulty of making sweeping generalizations about Companions, like the misconception that all or most of them supported Uthman's policies. For example, Ibn Udays was a Companion who pledged allegiance under the tree, or Bayat al-Ridhwan, an event praised in the Qur'an (Q48:18).

After the killing of Uthman, the people wanted Ali ibn Abi Talib (as) to become the leader and this news reached Aisha who was expecting her own cousin Talhah to come to power. In Tabari it is reported that Aisha said:

> I see Talhah has taken possession of the keys to the
> public treasuries and storehouses. If he becomes

caliph (after Uthman), he will follow the path of his parental cousin Abu-Bakr. Ibn Abbas said: 'O' Mother (of believers), if something happens to that man (i.e., Uthman), people would seek asylum only with our companion (namely, Ali).' Aisha replied: 'Be quiet! I have no desire to defy or quarrel with you.'

Aisha accepted and propagated the fabricated accusations and rumours that Ali ibn Abi Talib (as) was culpable in Uthman's death. Her army believed Ali had either fraternized with Uthman's killers before the murder or allowed them into his army. Aisha rejected the legitimacy of Imam Ali's election and demanded an army to be raised to support the candidacy of her cousin Talhah and brother-in-law Zubayr. She raised an army of thousands, but no other wife of the Holy Prophet (pbuh) would join her. The only one who wanted to join her was Hafsa, Umar's daughter. But Abdullah ibn Umar would not allow her, saying that he would not join and therefore she had no permission to go either.

Aisha led the army with the intention of removing Imam Ali (as) himself from the caliphate or killing him. Talhah and Zubayr were her key allies. It is ironic that Zubayr was the first cousin of Ali ibn Abi Talib (as) and had once supported the Imam.

There is a *hadith* which says, a lady came to Aisha one day and said to her, "Aisha, what do you say about a mother who kills her child?"

She replied, "This lady goes straight to Hell." She said, "What do you say about a mother who killed all of her children, twenty thousand of them in one day?" What a tragedy that a woman honoured as a "Mother of the Believers" in the Quran was involved in twenty thousand deaths in the first ever civil war within the Muslim *ummah*. Imam Ali (as) begged Aisha, Talhah, and Zubayr not to proceed with the battle; it was unjust to have Muslims fighting Muslims. But they were adamant.

A youth accepted the duty from Imam Ali (as) to go with the Qur'an in his hands to call the opposition to fear Allah and spare each other any bloodshed. But they attacked and killed him, thus beginning the war. Imam Ali (as) presented his army, as was the custom, by openly identifying himself as the Commander of the armed forces, and on his right, Malik al-Ashtar, on his left, Muhammad ibn Abu Bakr, and in front of him was Ammar ibn Yasir.

When Aisha heard her brother's name, she called out to the people, "He dares to fight his sister." He said, "I will fight anyone who attacks my master." Imam Ali (as) and Malik al-Ashtar, absolutely annihilated the army, but needed to put an end to the bloodshed by cutting the legs of the camel, thus causing the opposition leader, Aisha, to fall.

Malik was ordered to go cut the legs of the camel, while Muhammad ibn Abu Bakr was sent to catch her as she fell. Aisha called out when he caught her, "Remove your hands from the body of the wife of the Holy Prophet (pbuh). How dare you touch me when you are not *mahram,* lawful, to me?"

The only man in Ali ibn Abi Talib's (as) army who was *mahram* to her was the one he sent to show respect to her when she fell on the ground. If it had been anyone else, she could have accused Imam Ali (as) of desecrating her honour and sanctity. She disparaged Muhammad ibn Abu Bakr for fighting against his own sister, but he replied to her that she was the one out of line as a rebel commander at war with the rightful leader. He made it clear to her that he neither had sympathy for her nor those who plotted with her.

Muhammad ibn Abu Bakr was twenty-six years old on the day of Jamal and only one year later Imam Ali (as) had decided that he should become governor of Egypt. At the age of twenty-seven the whole of Egypt was in Muhammad b. Abi Bakr's hands, and Imam Ali (as) reminded him in a letter:

> This is the commandment of Imam Ali ibn Abi Talib
> (as) to Muhammad ibn Abu Bakr. Fear Allah (swt)
> and obey him secretly and openly. I order you to
> treat Muslims leniently, the sinful Muslim intensely
> and the non-Muslim fairly. I also order you to give
> back the wrong their rights. Punish the wrong
> severely. Punish people, and do charitably as much as
> possible. Allah (swt) will reward the charitable and
> will punish the sinful. I order you to call people who
> are under His power to obey Allah (swt) and to be

united. If they do so, they will gain good health and reward that are too great to be estimated. I order you to behave modestly with the people…Regard the close and the remote equally. Judge among people with fear…

Thus he started his service with the fear of Allah and with the stable and balanced guidance of the rightful Imam.

Sometime later, Muhammad ibn Abu Bakr heard that Muawiyah was causing trouble for Imam Ali (as). He wrote him a phenomenal letter openly praising and supporting Imam Ali (as) and boldly declaring Muawiyah's illegitimacy. The reply from Muawiyah was threatening, but also quite revealing. Muhammad ibn Abu Bakr wrote:

From Muhammad, son of Abu Bakr, to the sinner, Muawiyah, son of Sakhr. Peace of Allah (swt) on to those who obey Him, from one who is peaceful to whoever accepts only Allah (swt) as his Master. In His omnipotence, greatness, power, and might, Allah (swt) did not create the creation in vain, nor due to a weakness in Him. Nor does He possess a need for what He creates. Rather, He created His beings so that they may worship Him.

He lets some of them sin, while keeping others on the right guidance. Some of them He left to suffer. Some He granted happiness. Then He knowingly chose from them Muhammad (pbuh) to be the sole bearer of His message.

He selected him to receive His revelation and entrusted him to carry out His commands. He sent him as His Messenger, bearer of glad tidings and warner to testify to the divine books which were revealed before.

So he invited people to accept his mission through wisdom and beautiful exhortation. The first to respond positively to his call, to obey him, to believe him, to put his all at his disposal, and to be a Muslim was his brother and cousin, Ali (as). He believed in him with regard to the knowledge of the unknown.

He preferred him to everyone else he loved. He protected him with his own life. He solaced him in every precarious situation. He fought those whom he had fought, and sought peace with those with whom he was at peace. He never fled when death was imminent out of his love for his life. He came out as one unmatched in power.

Nobody could ever come close to what he took. I saw how you tried to reach his status. Though you are what you are, while he is the one who stood out above the rest as the foremost in doing anything good.

His conviction was most sincere, his offspring, the best of all people, his wife, the best of all women, his cousin was the best, whose brother traded his life on the day of Mu' ta, his uncle, the master of martyrs, his father, Abu Talib, defended the Messenger (pbuh) of Allah (swt) in his mission.

Whereas you are the accursed and the son of the accursed. You and your father have never ceased plotting to undermine the religion of Allah (swt), trying both of you to put out the light of Allah (swt), rallying others behind you, spending your wealth and seeking the support of other tribes.

Thus did your father die, and in his footsteps you are now following. Those who testify against you are the very ones whom you seek to please, while those who resort to you are the pariahs from the remnants of parties, the leaders of hypocrisy, those who are the foremost in dissenting from the Messenger of Allah (pbuh).

Those who testify for Ali (as), though his virtues are quite obvious, are his supporters whom Allah (swt) mentioned and praised in the Qur'an over all the Muhajirs and the Ansars: they are with him; battalions and valiant defenders, protecting with their words, ready to spill their blood for him.

Woe unto you! How dare you compare yourself as an
equal to Ali ibn Abi Talib (as) while he is the
representative of the Holy Prophet (pbuh), his *wasi*,
the father of his offspring.

Enjoy your life as long as you can through the means
of your falsehood, and let the son of al-Aas support
your sinning, for your end seems to have come close,
and your mischief seems to be waning: soon you will
come to know who is to receive the lofty rewards!

What a powerful letter defending the Imam and clarifying truth
from falsehood, what clear evidence that this man stood by the Holy
Prophet (pbuh) and his rightful successor! Muhammad ibn Abu Bakr
was fearless and bold against injustice and didn't flinch when he
became further exposed for this open opposition.

Muawiyah's reply is arguably the most deadly and cunning
paragraphs in Islamic history. It is notable how Muawiyah revealed
his and his family's vitriolic jealousy of Imam Ali (as) and was even
insulting to Allah (swt). What is so striking as well is the revelatory
nature of the letter where he clearly and openly identifies the previous
caliphs as the role models for opposing Ali in Islamic history:

I received your letter wherein you state Allah (swt) has
indicated of His Greatness, Might, and Omnipotence
and what He bestowed upon the Messenger of Allah
(pbuh), in addition to a great deal of talk which you
authored to your own whims. Such talk is shameful

for you and offensive to your father. In it you stated the merits of the son of Abu Talib (as) and his age-old feats and kinship to the Messenger of Allah (pbuh), his having supported and looked after the Prophet (pbuh) in every precarious situation.

Your argument against me was produced by praising someone else rather than demonstrating your own merits; so you should praise the Lord Who has deprived you of these merits and gave them to someone else. During the lifetime of Holy Prophet (pbuh), your father and I used to recognize the merits of Abu Talib's son and the fact that his feats were greater than ours.

When Allah (swt) chose [death] for His Prophet (pbuh), completing His promise to him, your father and his Farooq were the first to snatch rights away from Ali. This is something they both agreed upon. They coordinated. Then they invited him to swear the oath of allegiance, but he slackened and was hesitant, so they harboured evil intentions against him and plotted to kill him. It was then, he swore the oath of allegiance to them.

Then the third person, Uthman, stood up to follow their (Abu Bakr and Umar's) guidance and walk in

their footsteps, whereupon you and your friend
faulted him for doing so.

So be on your guard, O son of Abu Bakr, for you will
see the evil of your affair. And do measure your span
according to your own measure: you will neither
equal nor parallel one whose vision weighs as much as
a mountain.

The cunning remarks Muawiyah made in this letter would
shatter a man whose ego was weak and easily threatened, but not
Muhammad ibn Abu Bakr. Muawiyah tried to shift the blame for his
own usurpation to the origins of it, as if that somehow legitimized the
perpetuation of wrongdoing or relieved him of his crime. But he
tried to throw some culpability onto Abu Bakr because of
Muhammad b. Abi Bakr's kinship to his father.

This exchange opened the door of vindictiveness and war. Amr
ibn al-Aas fought desperately to win the governorship of Egypt back
from ibn Abī Bakr. Amr ibn al-Aas plotted with Muawiyah to strip
this upstart of his position, vowing to do whatever Muawiyah
commanded. They began to plot his demise, and amassed an army of
six thousand soldiers to overtake Egypt.

Imam Ali (as) became aware of their plotting; Muhammad ibn
Abu Bakr wrote him saying the situation was precarious. Imam Ali
(as) told him to mobilize the four thousand soldiers in Egypt. Imam
Ali (as) sent Malik al-Ashtar to take up the reigns of Egypt and to
support Muhammad ibn Abu Bakr. Malik al-Ashtar was the nemesis

of Muawiyah and was a feared and extraordinarily capable fighter and leader, the only way to overcome him would be through trickery and underhandedness. On his journey, he was poisoned at an inn and this left Egypt and Muhammad ibn Abu Bakr vulnerable. The forces of Amr ibn al-Aas forces were stronger and they successfully defeated ibn Abu Bakr's men. Muhammad ibn Abu Bakr managed to escape until the volatile and vicious Muawiyah ibn Hudayj caught him and killed him. To disgrace him further, under the orders of Amr ibn al-Aas, ibn Hudayj took Muhammad's dead body and forced it into the stomach of a donkey.

This abject and detestable Muawiyah ibn Hudayj had the donkey's skin stitched back up with the body of Muhammad ibn Abu Bakr firmly inside it. Now this is not the only the evil and degraded act he committed, after this he had the body of the donkey completely burned. What oppression the companions of Ahl al-Bayt (as) faced throughout history!

Imam Ali (as) was overcome and distraught; the cruelty of his rivals was extreme and evil through and through. He described how he had lost his son - Muhammad ibn Abu Bakr and prayed that Allah (swt) bestow blessings and mercy on his soul. But the tragedy of his death doesn't end there. Today in Cairo if one wants to go and visit Muhammad ibn Abu Bakr's grave, one would be hard-pressed to find anyone who even knows his name, let alone where he is buried. But shockingly, one of the largest mosques and the oldest in the entire African continent is the Mosque of Amr ibn al-Aas.

He is falsely given the title of "Conqueror of Egypt." However, such a title does not befit someone who allegedly exposed his private parts in the Battle of Siffin, so Imam Ali (as) would spare him a final deathblow. This grand mosque was established ten years after the Holy Prophet's (pbuh) death at the time of Amr ibn al-Aas' conquest of Egypt under Umar. Sadly, the grave of Muhammad ibn Abu Bakr is on a road of mechanic shops, with spare parts, black oil, and rubbish about.

While Amr ibn al-Aas has a thousand people at his grave saying, "May Allah (swt) be pleased with him" after mentioning his name. The grave of Muhammad ibn Abu Bakr has a plaque inside a small mosque which reads, "Muhammad, son of Abu Bakr" with few visitors to remember his great sacrifices. May the followers of Aal Muhammad (as) have the honour to be alongside the few and the distinguished Companions and keep their noble histories alive.

Works Cited

Humphreys, R. Stephen. Trans. *The History of al-Tabari, Vol. 15, The Crisis of the Early Caliphate: The Reign of 'Uthman A.D. 644-656/A.H. 24-35.* New York: SUNY Series in Near Eastern Studies, 1990.

Rizvi, Sayyid Muhammad. *Islam: Faith, Practice & History.* Qom: Ansariyan Publications, 2004.

The Holy Qur'an: Text, Translation and Commentary. Trans. Abdullah Yusuf Ali. Brentwood, MD: Amana Corporation. 1989.

Chapter 6:

Ja'far ibn Abi Talib

J a'far ibn Abi Talib occupies a prominent position in Islamic history as one of the greatest Companions of the Holy Prophet Muhammad (pbuh). When one examines Islamic history, there are few who come near the merits that he earned in his lifetime. However, what is unfortunate is that Ja'far ibn Abi Talib is very much an understudied figure in many of the Muslim communities today. It is rare to find a book on the biography of Ja'far ibn Abi Talib in the English language, and in the Arabic language not more than two or three books were written about him in the past three to four hundred years. Therefore, there is a need for the Muslim community to discover the biography of this great personality.

As a precedent, the Qur'an continuously stresses to always keep a relationship with those great personalities who came before. For example, there are numerous verses that state, "*wadhkur fi al-kitab*", and "Remember in the book…" and then there is the name of a personality. Sometimes it may say "*wadhkur fi al-kitab Ismail…wadhkur fi al-kitab Idris…wadhkur fi al-kitab Zakariya.*" Part of the ethos of the Qur'an is the constant reminder to believers to have a relationship with those personalities who came before. Second, by exploring the biography of personalities like Ja'far ibn Abi

Talib's we are able to recognise in him a realistic role model for the religion.

As one can tell from his title, he was the son of Abu Talib and Fatimah bint Asad. Abu Talib had four sons and two daughters. His two daughters were Fakhitah and Jumana. The eldest son was Talib, then Aqil, Ja'far, and Ali (as). Between each of these four sons, there was a ten-year age gap. Talib is not mentioned much in Islamic literature but what is known about him is that he died at the age of fifty-five and he was forced to fight in the Battle of Badr, but managed to leave the opposition army and return back home.

Aqil was a famous son of Abu Talib and was ten years younger than Talib. He lived until the age of ninety and was a beloved figure to the extent that the Holy Prophet (pbuh) was once asked about him. The Holy Prophet (pbuh) said, "I told Aqil, son of Abu Talib, oh Aqil, I love you because of two reasons. First, I love you for who you are. Second, I love you because my uncle Abu Talib used to love you." No doubt, Divine love for Aqil was compounded because he would have sons who would die alongside the Prophet's grandson Hussain (as) at the Battle of Karbala.

The third son, who was ten years younger than Aqil, was Ja'far and from the beginning of his life, he had certain noble attributes. The person who physically resembled the Holy Prophet (pbuh) the most from the sons of Abu Talib was Ja'far. Furthermore, an important point about Ja'far is that he was the first of the sons of Abu Talib to be raised alongside the Holy Prophet (pbuh) and to follow him in each of his attributes. Normally one hears that Ali ibn Abi Talib (as) was brought up by the Holy Prophet (pbuh) and of that there is no doubt.

However Ja'far ibn Abu Talib also benefitted from this special connection and it helped form his character and personality in blessed ways. From the time of his childhood, Ja'far would observe his father's love and sacrifices for the Holy Prophet (pbuh). In the traditions, he describes how his mother and father would take care of every need of the Holy Prophet (pbuh) during his early years including the arrangement of his (pbuh) marriage proposal.

Ja'far narrates, "I was five years old when I witnessed the *nikah* of the Prophet (pbuh) to Sayedah Khadijah (as)." Abu Talib, the father of Ja'far, read the blessed *nikah* of the Holy Prophet (pbuh) to Khadijah (as) indicating that all of them were monotheistic believers.

It is also known from Ja'far's reports that he would follow the Holy Prophet (pbuh) wherever he would go, and certainly this attachment had an effect on the personality of this young Ja'far.

A famous *hadith* from Imam Ali (as) says, "I used to follow the Holy Prophet (pbuh) like a she-camel's child follows the she-camel." Ja'far, before Imam Ali (as), used to follow the Holy Prophet (pbuh) in the same manner. There is a narration in relation to this affectionate connection between the Holy Prophet (pbuh) and Ja'far from Imam al-Baqir (as):

> The Holy Prophet (pbuh) one day came to Ja'far and
> said, 'Oh Ja'far, my Lord has said to me that He loves

you because of four reasons.' Ja'far looked at the
Holy Prophet (pbuh) and replied, 'Oh Holy Prophet
(pbuh), what are these four?' He said, 'My Lord
revealed to me I love Ja'far ibn Abi Talib for four
things which he never did, which others were doing in
their youth in the Ayyam al-Jahiliyyah, Age of
Ignorance. My Lord says to me that I love Ja'far
because in the Ayyam al-Jahiliyyah, while other
youths were drinking alcohol, Ja'far never drank.
While other youths were lying, Ja'far never lied.
While other youths were committing adultery, Ja'far
never committed adultery. While other youths were
worshipping idols, Ja'far never worshipped idols.
Ja'far replied to this revelation from the Holy Prophet
(pbuh) by saying, 'Oh Holy Prophet (pbuh), do you
know why I stayed away from these four? I remained
away from worshipping an idol because there is no
point in worshipping that which can neither benefit
me, nor harm me. I never drank alcohol because
alcohol inhibits the rationality of the human being. I
never lied because lying reduces from the valour and
bravery of a human being. I never committed
adultery, because I feared that act would come back
and haunt me and my family with its consequences.'
(al-Saduq, *Man la yahduruhu al-faqih,* 4:397)

Allah (swt) loves a youth when he or she stays away from these things at a young age. Passions are greater and temptations are more appealing and then they cool with old age. Certainly it is easier for anyone to become religious later in life - once all the fun has been had, all the vices have been tried, and all the temptations indulged. In old age, the end of life and the spectre of the grave loom large and these realities sober the desires.

The effect of peer pressure is not a new phenomena and the Holy Prophet (pbuh) made a point about how Ja'far successfully overcame it even in the deserts of Arabia through the use of his faith and intellect. His love for Allah (swt) was his primary motivation to be moral, but his faith was not separate from the use of his intellect and logical thought processes. Ja'far did not choose to overcome these vices simply out of fear of what others would think, but chose instead to understand the rationale and weigh the consequences.

He showed mature critical-thinking skills. In honour of this colossal spiritual achievement the Holy Prophet (pbuh) had a *hadith* where he said, "The best of the people in their behaviour, were Hamzah, Ali, and Ja'far."

One famous incident indicates that Ja'far became a pillar of the religion at its most nascent stage. Abu Talib described how one day he was walking with Ja'far and saw the Holy Prophet (pbuh) praying with two people accompanying him. Abu Talib mentions in his narration that the one in front of them was his nephew Muhammad (pbuh), and behind him was Ali (as), and then Khadijah (as). Then he looked at Ja'far and he told him to go become a wing alongside his Prophet (pbuh) in prayer.

That was the triumvirate of the first followers of Muhammad (pbuh) in the early days of the religion of Islam: Ali (as), Ja'far, and Khadijah (as). They were the core, and with time more followers came to the religion such as Ammar ibn Yasir, Abu Dhar al-Ghaffari, Zayd, Bilal, and Ammar's parents. As word spread about the religion and the number of its followers began to increase, the Quraysh became harsher with these Companions of the Holy Prophet (pbuh).

The Quraysh were the elite royalty in Mecca. They suddenly saw this orphan Muhammad (pbuh) taking all of their sons away from them, turning their slaves against them, and challenging their way of life. They began to torture anyone who was found to be following this religion in an effort to put a stop to this insurgency, regardless of which tribe they belonged.

Ammar ibn Yasir was taken and tortured. His father Yasir and his mother Sumayyah were tortured and killed. Bilal al-Habashi was taken and tortured, and others as well. The Holy Prophet (pbuh) was well aware of how these early believers were suffering and how the religion was being threatened. He developed a plan to protect the early believers and to provide them with the opportunity to practice the religion free from harm.

The Holy Prophet (pbuh) called them together to discuss his plan for them to obtain the rights to freedom of expression and belief in a land governed by a king who followed Divine scripture. Once they were all gathered, he looked around at his Companions comprising of eleven men and four women.

Amongst the men were Uthman ibn Affan, Uthman ibn Mathun, Zubayr ibn Awwam, and amongst the women was his stepdaughter Ruqayyah. He (as) described how distressed he was about their hardship and pain and that he wanted to relieve the pressure the early converts were facing. He told them of the region called Abyssinia, where there was a Christian emperor who did not differentiate amongst the people on the basis of their religion, but rather looked for the good principles in any human being.

That Christian emperor, also called Najashi or Negus, would be able to provide asylum to this budding group of Muslims. However, this trip required them to leave their homeland, their families, and the comforts of life, for the sake of spreading and protecting the religion of Islam. There was a ship setting sail that could take them from the Hijaz towards Abyssinia. Upon arriving in Abyssinia, they were to present a letter to the Najashi which read:

> In the Name of Allah, the Most Merciful, Most
> Gracious, From Muhammad, the Messenger of Allah
> to the Negus Al-Asham, king of Abyssinia. Peace, I
> praise Allah, who is the King, the Holy, the Peace, the
> Faithful, the Watcher, and I bear witness that Jesus,
> son of Mary, is the Spirit of Allah and His Word,
> Which He cast to Mary the virgin, the good, the pure,
> so that she conceived Jesus. Allah created him from

His Spirit and His Breathing as He created Adam by His Hand and His Breathing. I call you to Allah, the Unique without partner, and to His obedience, and to follow me and believe in that which came to me, for I am the Messenger of Allah. I have sent to you my cousin Ja'far with a number of Muslims, and when they come, entertain them without haughtiness, for I invite you and your armies to Allah. I have accomplished my work and my admonition, so receive my advice. Peace upon all those that follow True Guidance.

This group of eleven men and four women migrated in the fifth year of the Prophethood of the Holy Prophet (pbuh) when he was forty-five years of age. This was to be known as the first *hijrah*, or migration, in Islam. When they reached Abyssinia, they took the letter to the Najashi and found that he was willing to provide them with sanctuary from the oppression they had faced in their own land.

They expected him to ask questions about their beliefs and religion, but he conveyed to them that under his rule and in his land anyone being oppressed was welcome regardless of their religion. They stayed in that land for a year but eventually became homesick. A rumour came to them that the Quraysh in Mecca had not only made peace with the Holy Prophet (pbuh), but that all the Quraysh had become Muslims. Uthman ibn Affan, with his wife Ruqayyah, Uthman ibn Mathun, Zubayr ibn Awwam, made preparations and boarded the ship to return to the Hijaz and then journeyed on to Mecca.

On their return journey to Mecca, they were on the outskirts of the city when they met one of the Muslims. They told him they had come from Abyssinia and while peacefully living there they heard that the Holy Prophet (pbuh) had now been given sanctuary and they desired to return home.

The Muslim replied that in fact that rumour was false, on the contrary the Holy Prophet (pbuh) was under even more pressure; he advised them to return to the safe-haven they had found in Abyssinia. Having heard this disappointing news the historical report suggests either the migrants met with the Holy Prophet (pbuh) for a short period or changed course and returned back to Africa without arriving in Mecca

This was one of the hardest periods for the Holy Prophet (pbuh) since there was an intense economic and social boycott of the Muslims. They retreated to a rocky ravine area known as the Shi'b Abu Talib. No one was allowed to sell any goods to Muhammad (pbuh) or his followers, or engage in any social connections or contracts.

The Holy Prophet (pbuh), recognizing his young community was threatened once again, sent an even larger delegation to Abyssinia to seek asylum. Eighty-three men and eighteen women were in this second delegation that left in the sixth year of Islam. For a second time, some narrations report the Holy Prophet (pbuh) selected his cousin, Ja'far ibn Abi Talib, as their leader. The Prophet (pbuh) described him as the most articulate, knowledgeable, and diplomatic amongst his Companions.

These attributes were all necessary to present the religion of Islam to the Abyssinians and foster good relations with them. Ja'far prepared to leave his homeland and family yet again. Now he had to leave his ailing father whom he would not see alive again.

One can only hope that today's Muslim followers of the Ahl al-Bayt (as) would have enough devotion and commitment to answer Imam al-Mahdi's (atfs) call if he asked the same. Ja'far was willing to give his life as a sacrifice for the religion's growth and protection, and he listened to the Holy Prophet's advice about what to discuss with the Najashi upon their next meeting.

Ja'far led the delegation that left in the middle of the night; again his devoted and self-sacrificing wife, Asma bint Umays, accompanied him. Indeed, she is considered one of the greatest ladies in Islamic history. When news of their departure to Africa reached the Quraysh, they were angered and were even more desperate to put a stop to the religion.

They were enraged that Muhammad (pbuh) thought that he could send a delegation of his (Meccan) followers to Africa and spread his religion that went against the age-old tradition of the Meccans. So Abu Jahl and Abu Sufyan asked two men to go the Najashi and put a stop to this on-going threat from the young Muslim community there.

They appointed Amr ibn al-Aas and Abdullah ibn Rabi'ah who were laden with gifts, some very unique, for the emperor, but Abu Jahl was cunning; he knew the emperor would not be easily impressed with worldly gifts like some of the guards or low-level priests of the church. Abu Jahl advised them to tell the emperor that not only have these refugees left the traditions of their forefathers and caused unrest between family members, but their beliefs criticized Christian belief in the divinity of Jesus.

Amr ibn al-Aas (who later plotted and schemed with Muawiyah against the Ahl al-Bayt (as)), was not a simple politician, but the master of cunningness. Amr ibn al-Aas and Abdullah ibn Rabi'ah arrived in Abyssinia, and no sooner did they enter the grand church, they demanded an appointment with the Najashi.

They were told by the officials that the Najashi was unavailable, but the two didn't take no for an answer and began to show the gifts they had brought. The officials were not impressed, but eventually there was one gift that got their attention, and it was a group of beautiful Arabian women. This gift apparently opened the door immediately for Amr ibn al-Aas and Abdullah ibn Rabi'ah, who were given an audience with the Najashi.

After introducing themselves, they declared their business; they had come to tell him about the fugitives who had come to his land from Mecca. The Najashi was not readily convinced by the claims of Amr ibn al-Aas that the group consisted of criminals. He had granted them asylum from oppression and found that they had lived peaceably in his land.

Amr ibn al-Aas continued to press his point, saying they hadn't been oppressed but were troublemakers in the land of Mecca, that they were challenging the belief of their forefathers. He said they had been causing havoc in their town preaching a new religion.

The Najashi questioned his claim that they were the ones causing destruction in their land; on the contrary they were the ones receiving the hardship. Amr ibn al-Aas denied these points with a slick tongue, insisting that he and his party were not the type to oppress others. The Najashi called Ja'far ibn Abi Talib to be brought into the court to hear his claims alongside these accusations.

He asked if it was true that they had caused destruction in their land. Ja'far went on to explain that the community originally practiced idol worship, and that some amongst them had come to worship the One God. He explained how their morals had been elevated, that prior to this new way the people of Mecca were prone to steal, but now they honoured their trusts. It was customary for men to bury their daughters alive, but now they raised their daughters with the same rights as their sons. He explained how their Prophet Muhammad (pbuh) had taught them that the white man and the black man are equal in the eyes of God.

Ja'far was eloquent and connected with the Najashi on their shared common principles of morality. He focused on their shared beliefs although they practiced different religions. He went on to explain how the religion of Muhammad (pbuh) was one that believed in the Lord of Adam (pbuh), the Lord of Noah (pbuh), Abraham (pbuh), Moses (pbuh), and Jesus (pbuh). At the mention of Jesus's (pbuh) name, the Najashi was very intrigued and pleased. Ja'far was successful in his address. Najashi granted them continued sanctuary in his land.

The two parties were dismissed after his ruling, but Amr ibn al-Aas did not give up that easily and came back the following day, asking to speak with the Najashi once more. He asked the emperor if he realised that although they claimed to believe in Jesus (pbuh), that they didn't believe he was the son of God, and furthermore these fugitives believed he was the servant of God and Muhammad (pbuh) was greater than him.

He managed to convince the emperor to further question the asylum seekers about how they didn't believe in Jesus (pbuh) as the saviour of mankind, planting a seed of doubt in the Najashi. Amr ibn al-Aas had nothing to do with Jesus (pbuh), nothing to do with Muhammad (pbuh), nothing to do with spirituality and religion, but he made it seem as though he was there to protect the virtue of the Christian's belief in Jesus (pbuh). His actions were all just political manoeuvres.

The Najashi had Ja'far brought before him again and asked him to explain the Muslim's belief in Jesus (pbuh). Ja'far said that they believed he was a servant based on the chapter named after his mother, Mary (as) in the Holy Qur'an, where in fact her name is mentioned more than in the Bible.

The Najashi asked him to recite verses of the Qur'an that refer to Christ and Mary, whereupon Ja'far recited the verses from the chapter about Mary (as). The chapter describes how God favoured her, how Jesus (pbuh) was the spirit of God breathed into the womb of Mary (as), and how his blessed birth took place. The emperor was particularly interested to hear about his birth and how Jesus (pbuh) spoke at birth to defend his virgin mother because the Bible does not mention these details. He prompted Ja'far to tell him the words of Jesus (pbuh), which he did. He said:

> In the name of Allah, the most Beneficent, the most Merciful. [Jesus said] "I am indeed a servant of God: He hath given me revelation and made me a prophet; And He hath made me blessed wheresoever I be, and hath enjoined on me Prayer and Charity as long as I live; (He) hath made me kind to my mother, and not overbearing or miserable; So peace is on me the day I was born, the day that I die, and the day that I shall be raised up to life (again). (Q19. 30-33)

The Najashi looked at Amr ibn al-Aas, and then he looked at the ground, took a stick and drew a line across the ground. He said, "The difference between my religion and the religion of Muhammad (pbuh) is the length of this line here." At that he asked Amr ibn al-

Aas and Abdullah ibn Rabi'ah to leave his land and allowed the Muslims to remain in Abyssinia in peace.

Ja'far ibn Abi Talib and the other Muslims were now free and over the following years established the foundations of Islam in Africa. Ja'far and his wife Asma had three children in Africa and the first Muslim to be born in Africa was Abdullah ibn Ja'far, the future husband of Sayedah Zaynab (as). Ja'far ibn Abi Talib had two other sons, Muhammad and Aun.

Aun would eventually marry Umm Kulthum (as), the daughter of Imam Ali (as). Ja'far ibn Abi Talib himself used to say, "My sons are for the daughters of Ali (as)." Because of this migration to Africa, many Muslim communities were established and the wives of many of the future Imams of the Ahl al-Bayt (as) came from Africa. Consider the fact that all the Imams(as) from Imam al-Sadiq (as) until Imam al-Hadi (as), had wives from Africa.

Ja'far ibn Abi Talib laid the seeds for Islam in Abyssinia, and that is why today's Ethiopia (part of historic Abyssinia), still has a large Muslim population. In fact Ethiopia has the third largest Muslim population in Africa after Nigeria and Egypt,. Twenty-five million Muslims are the *sadaqah jariah*, the perpetual charity, of Ja'far ibn Abi Talib such that every time the *shahadah* is recited, "I bear witness that there is no god but Allah (swt), I bear witness that Muhammad (pbuh) is His messenger" in Africa, the *thawab*, blessing, goes to Ja'far.

The Najashi, who was such a pious and just man, also converted to Islam. The Holy Prophet (pbuh) wrote him a letter saying:

In the name of Allah, the most Beneficent, the most Merciful. Oh Najashi, you are a Christian priest who has been hospitable to us. You gave us sanctuary when others kicked us out. You gave us honour when nobody showed any respect towards us. But oh Najashi, I invite you towards the word of the final messenger of God. I am Muhammad (pbuh), in the line of Jesus (pbuh) and Moses (pbuh) and Abraham (pbuh) and Noah (pbuh). If you believed in Moses's (pbuh) miracles and Jesus's (pbuh) miracles, then you will believe in my message as well. Oh Najashi, accept the invitation to Islam.

The emperor announced to his people that regardless of whether they joined him or not, he was convinced that Muhammad's (pbuh) religion was the religion of God and that he would become a Muslim.

As soon as he became a Muslim, the Holy Prophet (pbuh) gave him the honourable invitation of reciting the Holy Prophet's (pbuh) *nikah* to the daughter of Abu Sufyan. Umm Habibah, the daughter of Abu Sufyan, had married a Muslim man called Ubaydallah ibn Jahsh and also settled in Africa with the asylum seekers.

Her husband left the religion for an Abyssinian woman, with whom he had become infatuated, abandoning Umm Habibah. This daughter of Abu Sufyan already risked so much by joining the Holy

Prophet's (pbuh) religion, and now someone who was supposed to be an adherent to the religion disgracefully abandoned her. For sure, she would be mocked by the pagan Meccans and never taken back by her father.

The Holy Prophet (pbuh) ordered his marriage to Umm Habibah to be officiated by the Najashi in spite of his inability to travel to Abyssinia. Thus, the marriage contract was completed with the Najashi acting as the representative of the Prophet (pbuh). By completing the marriage in this way, the Prophet protected her from anyone taking advantage of her and ensured she would be looked after.

Allah (swt) revealed the following verse from the Qur'an about the Najashi:

> In the name of Allah, the most Beneficent, the most Merciful...And nearest among them in love to the believers wilt thou find those who say, We are Christians: because amongst these are men devoted to learning and men who have renounced the world, and they are not arrogant. And when they listen to the revelation received by the Messenger, thou wilt see their eyes overflowing with tears, for they recognise the truth: they pray: Our Lord! we believe; write us down among the witnesses. What cause can we have not to believe in Allah and the truth which has come

to us, seeing that we long for our Lord to admit us to

the company of the righteous? (Q5.82-84)

Although an emperor, the Najashi was a humble priest, a man of God and his heart was ripe for the words of Allah.

During Ja'far's time in Africa, many developments took place amongst the Muslims in Arabia. For example, seven years following his arrival in Africa, the Holy Prophet (pbuh) migrated to Medina and after many momentous events and battles, another seven years passed and it was the time of the Battle of Khaybar. The Holy Prophet (pbuh) had not seen Ja'far for fourteen years and he wrote to the Najashi asking him to send Ja'far ibn Abi Talib back towards Medina.

Once again Ja'far ibn Abi Talib was asked to sacrifice all that he had established in Africa and once again leave his family and his home, which he obediently did. At Khaybar after Ali ibn Abi Talib (as) had completely destroyed the opposition and earned every, the Holy Prophet saw from a distance a man walking towards him, and he recognized Ja'far ibn Abi Talib. He was so overjoyed that he announced to the whole community, "I don't know which one gives us greater joy, the victory of Ali (as) at Khaybar, or the return from Africa of Ja'far." The Holy Prophet (pbuh) gave such love and honour to Ja'far even at the moment of his brother Ali's (as) greatest victory.

Within the first couple of weeks of Ja'far's return from Africa he got a nickname, "Abul Masakin," the father of the needy. Abu

Hurayrah, who was from Ashab al-Suffah, the poor Companions who used to sleep in the mosque of the Holy Prophet and wait for charitable food to be distributed. He was the one to narrate the story of how Ja'far got this nickname.

Abu Hurayrah said that he used to go to Ja'far ibn Abi Talib with the pretence of asking a *fiqh*, jurisprudential, question, but he would pretend to forget his question. Before answering his question, Ja'far would then invite him for dinner at his home.

Thus Ja'far ibn Abi Talib became known as Abul Masakin. Ja'far was like all of the members of his family, from Abu Talib, to Ali (as), to Aqil who looked after the needy; every single one of them was the father of the needy.

But Ja'far ibn Abi Talib desired to be of even greater service and said to the Holy Prophet (pbuh):

> Oh Holy Prophet (pbuh), my brother (Ali (as)) annihilated the opposition at Badr, destroyed the opposition at Khandaq, and at Khaybar none could come near him. Oh Holy Prophet (pbuh), give me an opportunity in which I can defend the religion of Islam. I was there in Africa, but you haven't allowed me the chance to rise against any form of oppression that is happening to innocent people.

A year after he returned from Africa, Ja'far was presented with the opportunity to fight against oppression. The Holy Prophet (pbuh) had sent an ambassador by the name of Haarith ibn Umayr to go and meet the Roman emperor. The Roman emperor met him and asked his business. Haarith told him he had come with a letter with an invitation for him to convert to Islam.

The emperor was not like his counterpart in Abyssinia, on the contrary he was antagonistic and had Haarith beheaded. The head was sent back with the threat that any further envoys would meet the same fate. The Holy Prophet (pbuh) was grieved by this reaction to his letter which was a peaceful invitation to a religion and not a political threat or act of aggression. The Prophet's response was to raise an army to respond to this injustice.

He ordered three thousand soldiers to go towards the area of Mu' ta on the border of Jordan and Saudi Arabia with Ja'far ibn Abi Talib at the lead. Then the Holy Prophet (pbuh) appointed two more individuals to take the lead if the leader should fall, and they were Zayd ibn Haarithah and Abdullah ibn Rawahah. One of the soldiers present at these directives raised concern when he noticed that the Holy Prophet (pbuh) appointed more than one leader; he claimed that these three were going to die as *shahid*, or martyrs because the Holy Prophet (pbuh) always seemed to know when to appoint a certain number of leaders for a battle. When the Muslim forces confronted the Roman army, they were outnumbered four to one.

One of the Companions, who is often revered in other schools, expressed doubt about the confrontation wondering if their small contingent would be in jeopardy. Ja'far ibn Abi Talib replied, "There is no doubt in my heart. If we win, Allah (swt) has been good to us, and if we die as martyrs, Allah (swt) is also pleased with us for we have died in a cause against injustice."

Zayd ibn Haarithah was a bit doubtful as well, but Abdullah ibn Rawahah knew that they had come to fight against injustice and ensure the continued existence of the Muslim community. Ja'far ibn Abi Talib fought a valiant fight and that would be replicated by a brave warrior of his lineage in the future.

Abdullah ibn Umar ibn Khattab narrated that he saw Ja'far ibn Abi Talib laying on the ground with fifty-three arrows embedded in his body, but before Ja'far fell he observed Ja'far display tenacity that he had never seen before in a warrior. He described how Ja'far was attacked from behind and had his right hand chopped off, but he exclaimed aloud that he would continue the fight to defend this religion.

The enemy came and struck his other hand, and then he was besieged and fell to the ground with an arrow piercing his eye. Back in Medina the Holy Prophet (pbuh) was praying his *salah* and when he completed it, he looked up at the Companions present and told them, "Ja'far ibn Abi Talib has just lost his right hand, and has just lost his left. *Inna Lillah Wa Inna Illayhi Rajiun*, 'We belong to God and to Him is our return.' He has just been killed."

The Companions were astonished at this knowledge and the Holy Prophet (pbuh) told them to remain patient for when the soldiers returned they would confirm what he had said. He then left them and sought to be with his beloved daughter Fatimah al-Zahra (as).

The Holy Prophet (pbuh) asked her to accompany him to the house of Asma bint Umays. When they entered, Ja'far's children and their mother came forth, and the Holy Prophet (pbuh) began to stroke their heads. There is a *hadith* that says, "When one strokes the head of an orphan, for each hair that is stroked, it will be a light on the Day of Judgment."

Asma knew what this gesture meant, and she listened tearfully as the Holy Prophet (pbuh) described Ja'far's courageous and noble last moments. He (pbuh) consoled her and encouraged her not to worry, for Allah (swt) promised to replace Ja'far's hands with wings in Heaven, and that is why many people call him "Ja'far al-Tayyar", "Ja'far, the one who flies with wings." The Holy Prophet (pbuh) made preparations to conduct a *majlis* and invited the Muslim community to mourn for Ja'far ibn Abi Talib.

He then requested that his daughter Fatimah al-Zahra (as) prepare food. Thus began the tradition of food prepared as an honour for a person who has passed away, it is the *sunnah* of the Holy Prophet (pbuh). Abbas, the son of the 7th Imam, Imam al-Kadhim (as), asked his father the basis for the traditions of a *majlis*, regarding the mourning and the giving of food. His father informed him it was on the basis of what the Holy Prophet (pbuh) did in honour of Ja'far ibn Abi Talib.

Ja'far was buried in the land of Mu' ta far from his family. But the children of Ja'far and Asma remained close to their uncle Imam Ali (as) who would always indulge them. Abdullah, Ja'far's son, described how when he would beseech his uncle to buy him something and he refused, if he mentioned the name of his father he would be unable to refuse. Ali wished to always honour the memory of his martyred brother and his practice of caring for the orphans and the poor.

Before his martyrdom, Ja'far al-Tayyar was given a special gift from the Holy Prophet (pbuh) with such spiritual power that if recited every Friday, or every month, or even every year, it would erase a sin from ever existing for the reciter. This was an honour bestowed by the Holy Prophet (as) on Ja'far for his service in Africa. The supplication was given to Ja'far by the Holy Prophet (pbuh) when he saw him after the Battle of Khaybar.

It is a prayer of four cycles (*raka'at*), divided into two parts, prayed like the *salat al-fajr*. The worshipper recites surahs al-Zalzalah, al-Adiyat, al-Nasr, and al-Ikhlas after al-Faithah in each *rakah* respectively and the Tasbihaat al-Arbaa seventy-five times. The lovers of the Ahl al-Bayt (as) have the special privilege to honour what Ja'far ibn Abi Talib gave the religion of Islam and to recognize his legacy through this special devotional prayer.

Ja'far ibn Abi Talib's legacy carried on after his death and he was mentioned years after he died, even by the enemies of the Ahl al-Bayt (as). At Karbala, Imam Husayn (as) in his last moments came out in front of the battle field and addressed his attackers, "Oh army of Yazid, am I not the grandson of your Prophet (pbuh)? Am I not the nephew of your great uncle Hamzah? Is Ja'far not my uncle?"

And the reply of the jealous usurpers came forth under the blazing sun, "We acknowledge the Holy Prophet. We acknowledge [the piety of] Hamzah and Ja'far. But it is because of your father that we are killing you; to seek revenge against your father." Then in Shaam, Imam Zayn al-Abidin (as) stood in front of Yazid who was blatantly bragging about becoming the Muslim caliph and confronted him saying, "Allah (swt) has granted us six and given us excellence in seven. Allah has granted us knowledge, patience, eloquence, forbearance, courage, and the believer's love for us. Allah has given us seven in that from us is the Holy Prophet (pbuh), and from us is Hamzah, and from us is Ja'far ibn Abi Talib..."

Imam Zayn al-Abidin (as) one day remembered Abu Fadl Abbas and he said, "Allah (swt) has put mercy on my uncle Abbas. He altruistically sacrificed his life for his brother. Allah (swt) has given him wings in replacement of his hands, like Allah (swt) gave Ja'far ibn Abi Talib." But at least Ja'far ibn Abi Talib, when he fell to the ground, was buried soon after. Abu Fadl Abbas' holy body lay on the plains of Karbala for three nights with no one to bury him.

Ja'far ibn Abi Talib's body was collected together respectfully, whereas for Abbas, the enemy chopped the pieces of his body and scattered the pieces about. In Muharram the followers of the Ahl al-Bayt (as) must remember the story of Ja'far al-Tayyar and connect it with the story of Abbas; for Allah (swt) ensured history repeated itself in the sacrifice of Abbas and Ja'far al-Tayyar. They were two noble servants of Allah (swt) who embodied the unflinching spirit, courage, bravery, and everlasting commitment of true worshippers.

Works Cited

Muhammad ibn Ishāq, *Sira ibn Ishaq*. (Rabat: 1976).

Muhammad b. 'Abd Allāh Al-Ḥakim Naysābūrī. *Al-Mustadrak 'Alā Al-Ṣaḥīhayn*. (Beirut: 1986), vol 3, p.208-212.

Muhammad ibn 'Alī ibn Babawayh al-Ṣadūq. *Man Lā Yahduruhu Al-Faqīh*. (Qum: 1983).

Chapter 7:
Kumayl ibn Ziyad

Kumayl ibn Ziyad an-Nakha'i occupies a prominent position in Islamic history and is revered by many as one of the greatest companions of Imam Ali ibn Abi Talib (as). This companion was known to be the embodiment of dedication, sacrifice, valour, and loyalty. Few companions in the life of Imam Ali (as) possess a status and love for Ali ibn Abi Talib (as) like Kumayl ibn Ziyad. Indeed, few companions were seen with such reverence in the eyes of Imam Ali (as) like Kumayl.

If you look around the Muslim world today, over three hundred million Muslims on Thursday night remember this man's name in relation to a famous supplication. However, if one were to ask many of these observant Muslims who have read the supplication, or have fully memorized it, how much they know about the man behind the supplication, one would find that their knowledge would be limited at best.

This biography is a remedy to the paucity of knowledge about Kumayl ibn Ziyad who was alive at the time of the Holy Prophet (pbuh) although he did not meet him. He was a companion of Imam Ali ibn Abi Talib (as) and remained alongside the subsequent Imams (as) from Imam Hasan (as) to Imam al-Baqir (as), and also was alive for a brief period during the life of Imam al-Sadiq (as).

Kumayl ibn Ziyad was executed around 82 AH or shortly thereafter, so he died close to the age of ninety and lived a long life in pursuit of faith and justice.

Kumayl is noted throughout history for the depth of his spirituality, his courage, willingness to migrate for the sake of the religion of Islam, and the conviction to stand against tyrants. If one wants to recount one of the greatest stands against Hajjaj ibn Yusuf al-Thaqafi, the bloodthirsty and ruthless ruler of Iraq, then one should look at Kumayl. He is one of the few companions of Ali ibn Abi Talib (as) who is revered and respected by others even from different traditions. Many treatises have been written about him as well.

The Sufis have written one of their most famous treatises about Kumayl ibn Ziyad. The Baha'is consider Kumayl ibn Ziyad as one of their masters. Amongst the Shi'a, different schools have emerged that revere Kumayl. Therefore, it is an injustice if the followers of the Ahl al-Bayt (as) relegate this worthy personality to a simple mention on a Thursday night. The reality is that this man, like many of the great companions, is part of the reason why the lineage of the Ahl al-Bayt (as) has been preserved.

His full name was Kumayl ibn Ziyad al-Nakha'i from the Banu Nakha. His tribe was from the land of Yemen, although most people automatically assume that he was a Kufan for having lived in Iraq most of his life. The land of Yemen, until today, occupies a strategic position as an Islamic nation. Currently there is significant news about the political turmoil in Yemen, the people's drive for justice and human rights, protection of female minors, and economic stability.

People are continuing to face oppression, and many are standing up against injustice. The people of Yemen continue to have an unbelievable compassion for the Holy Prophet (pbuh) and his family (as), and often take the names of the beloved Ahl al-Bayt (as) such as Ali, Hasan, Husayn, Fatimah, and Zayn al-Abidin for their offspring.

The Shi'a are actually divided into a number of schools which includes the Zaydi school that is quite prevalent in Yemen in particular. There are also the Ismailis who accept all the Imams (as) up to and including Imam al-Sadiq (as) and then look to his son Ismail rather than Imam Musa ibn Ja'far (as) as the successor.

Then there are the Shi'a Ithna Ashari or the Twelvers who accept all twelve Imams (as) up to Imam Mahdi (atfs)[2]. There are nine million Zaydi Shi'a who accept the Imamate of Imam Ali, Hasan and Husayn and then those descendants of Fatima al-Zahra (as) who stand for justice and are knowledgeable jurists. The people of Yemen were originally introduced to Islam through Imam Ali (as).

The Holy Prophet (pbuh) had a strategic plan to send delegations out to different countries and nations whose people were warm and receptive to learn about the religion of Islam. This

---

[2] Ajjal Allahu Ta'ala Farajahu Sharif – May Allah the Most High hasten his noble reappearance.

outreach took place during a year called Aam al-Wufud, the Year of the Delegations (9AH/631CE) in which the Holy Prophet (pbuh) sent out ambassadors and countless delegations representing various tribes came to Medina to convert to Islam. The Prophet (pbuh) sent ambassadors to the people of Najran, Ta'if, the tribe of Thaqif, and the people of Tamim. Likewise, he sent a *wafid*, or delegate to the people of Yemen.

When the Holy Prophet (pbuh) sent a *wafid* to the people of Yemen, Kumayl was about nine or ten years old. According to calculations based on the narrations, Kumayl ibn Ziyad was born a year before the Hijrah of the Holy Prophet (pbuh) which means that by the time the Holy Prophet (pbuh) died, he would have been eleven.

Kumayl was born in Yemen, thus, he met the delegation of the Holy Prophet (pbuh) led by Khalid ibn Walid. Khalid ibn Walid was known for his prowess on the battlefield against the religion of Islam, especially on the day of Uhud. Were it not for the Holy Prophet (pbuh) and Imam Ali ibn Abi Talib (as), this religion would have died on the day of Uhud. Ali ibn Abi Talib (as) mustered the strength where he was able to defend himself against sixty-two soldiers on the mountain of Uhud defending the Holy Prophet (pbuh).

The extent of the fight left its marks and in a narration Fatimah al-Zahra (as) said, "We had just gotten married that year and I came to see his wounds after the battle of Uhud; there were sixty-three wounds on his body, but he remained standing."

This Khalid later became a Muslim and was sent to represent the religion to others. This role required a certain positive demeanour and ethic, as the representative could bring people towards the religion or repel them. Khalid stayed there amongst the people for a number of months. But it seemed the people of Yemen were not interested in converting.

The people were saying that although Khalid believed in Muhammad's (pbuh) religion, he didn't know much about it. He would encourage the people to believe and recite the *shahadah*, or testimony, to accept Islam. The Yemenis would ask him to explain more about the religion. He would mention the importance of the Qur'an and how central it was to read it. But when the people would ask more about the Qur'an, prayers and other obligations, they would not receive satisfying replies.

Although this Khalid ibn Walid joined the religion, he didn't have the capability to teach it properly, so the Holy Prophet (pbuh) called Imam Ali (as) and asked him to leave Medina for Yemen. He was to encounter the two main tribes there, Kumayl's tribe, the Nakha'is, and the Hamadanis.

The Nakha'is were known to be quite ferocious and would pelt stones at anyone they deemed unwelcome and the Hamadanis proved to be, after their conversion, the most loyal tribe to Aal Muhammad (as) during the lifetime of almost eight Imams (as). The poetry of

Abu al-Faras al-Hamadani attests to the intensity of this love and the sincerity of this tribe.

Imam Ali (as) arrived there in mid-winter, and as he approached their fortress, the Nakha'is all picked up stones and began pelting him. His companions on the journey were wondering what to make of this and what to do next, but he advised them to wait. One well-known Companion suggested they retaliate but Ali ibn Abi Talib (as) wouldn't allow it.

He advised patience, mentioning that the Yemeni tribe was still unfamiliar with Islam, and were weary of them as intruders. He reminded them that they might have had misconceptions about the religion. It was the obligation of the delegation to remove these misconceptions.

Eventually Imam Ali (as) was able to approach the tribe and begin a dialogue with them. They conveyed to him that they weren't interested in more ambassadors and that the one before was unable to explain anything of importance to them. Within a short while of Imam Ali's (as) orations regarding the religion, half of the Banu Nakha'i and Banu Hamadan became seriously interested. His title as the *Nahj al-Balaghah*, the *Peak of Eloquence*, was evident on this good-will trip; he had the greatest of gifts in speech and oration, his words had a precise impact and conveyed the best wisdom.

But whenever there is success, it inevitably threatens the one who didn't achieve that same success. One finds that this was the case with Imam Ali's (as) situation in Yemen. Because of the fame he achieved in Yemen, some Companions became upset and complained about him. Apparently the complaints reached the Holy Prophet's (pbuh) ears.

Kumayl was in Yemen, observing how Ali ibn Abi Talib (as) brought the guidance of Islam to his people. He was awe-struck by such an inspirational figure and vowed to himself that he would forever remain dedicated to such a noble leader, even if it meant migrating to a new city. Malik al-Ashtar and Uways al-Qarni did the very same thing. They left the vast, distant deserts of Yemen to be with Ali ibn Abi Talib (as) as devoted soldiers and companions.

When the disciples of Ali became prominent in Kufa, they were thought to have originated from there, but in actuality they were Yemeni youth who migrated to Kufa. Kumayl, at the age of twenty-five to thirty, travelled to be with Imam Ali (as) whom he accepted as his rightful leader and guide during the time of Uthman's caliphate. Whatever question he needed answered, whether legal, theological, or ethical, he would address them to Imam Ali (as) as would his companions, like Malik al-Ashtar, ibn Suhan, and Uways al-Qarani.

These companions were also aware of the political intrigues and injustices at the time, such as the appointment of Walid ibn Uqbah as governor of Kufa. He was Uthman's brother-in-law and the one the Holy Qur'an had pinpointed as an untrustworthy *fasiq*, evil-doer, during the time of the Holy Prophet (pbuh) in the following verse:

"O ye who believe! If a wicked person comes to you with any news, ascertain the truth, lest ye harm people unwittingly, and afterwards become full of repentance for what ye have done" (Q49:6).

Walid ibn Uqbah was named an evil-doer because of an incident with his former enemies, the Banu Mustaliq. He was appointed by the Prophet (pbuh) as a tax collector, but on his journey to collect their taxes, he decided against entering their land. He returned to the Prophet (pbuh) and instead of confessing to him that he never encountered them, he spun a dangerous tale in which he claimed they had apostatized and were intending to go to war against the Prophet (pbuh). Before any military engagements occurred, the Prophet received revelation clarifying Walid's lies.

Decades later, Walid led *salat al-fajr*, morning prayer, while drunk, going on to three and four units instead of two. Thus, noble companions of Imam Ali and other citizens of Kufa became outraged by the conduct of Uthman's appointee.

Kumayl was present at that *salat al-fajr* led by this complete destroyer of the religion. He observed Walid turn around and taunt the worshippers, "If you like, I can extend the prayer." What a mockery Walid ibn Uqbah was making of the religion and the post to which he was appointed. Kumayl, Malik al-Ashtar and about ten other of these young men, all around the age of thirty, led an uprising against this man.

They all stood up against Walid ibn Uqbah and he promptly had them removed from the city and sent to Shaam (Damascus). They stood up against Muawiyah, who was governor of Shaam at the time, and in the same vein as the scathing letter sent by Muhammad ibn Abu Bakr to Muawiyah, Kumayl ibn Ziyad exposed Muawiya's hypocrisy and illegitimacy. Kumayl was another thorn in the side of Muawiyah who cunningly claimed that Kumayl was causing disunity amongst Muslims when Allah (swt) specifically commands the community not to disunite.

Kumayl stunningly replied that protesting injustice is the prime obligation and Allah's (swt) religion is about justice, accountability, and ensuring those in power do not sow corruption in the land. Then Muawiyah thinking himself superior mentioned that Allah (swt) also says to obey Allah (swt), obey the Prophets (pbuh), and obey those in authority.

Kumayl confirmed that indeed he and his fellow protestors obey Allah (swt) and His Prophets (pbuh), but those in authority who were corrupt and illegitimate deserved no obedience. Muawiyah eventually had them exiled to Homs, but they were forced to leave there as well. They were men of justice, but men with no home.

Eventually, Kumayl suggested that he, Malik, and eight of their loyal companions go directly to Uthman, who had placed himself in a fine palace in Medina. They believed the Umayyads had obtained too many powerful positions in the government and were destroying the spirit of the religion of the Holy Prophet (pbuh).

When they arrived at his palace in Medina, Uthman ibn Affan greeted them with the greeting of peace, to which there was no reply. Kumayl and the group remained silent. Their silence spoke volumes regarding their disassociation from him. Uthman was utterly offended that they were not respecting him as caliph, but they refused and went on to declare their valid grievances against Walid ibn Uqbah, his illegitimate authority, his drunkenness, and his flagrant disregard for Islam. This confrontation was part of a series of events that ultimately led to Uthman's assassination.

When Imam Ali (as) became caliph thereafter, the civil unrest and attacks became absolutely overwhelming. Kumayl reported that those four and a half years of unrelenting pressure reached a level that affected him and his fellow supporters. The commonly accepted history glosses over the caliphate of Imam Ali (as) and the absolute injustice perpetuated against the most beloved personality to the Holy Prophet (pbuh). According to Ibn Majah's famous collection, the Holy Prophet (pbuh) once said, "Ali is from me and I am from him and no one represents me but Ali."

The so-called Muslims fought him in three extremely devastating and deadly civil wars in a period of only four years. It was a period of constant wars, first the Battle of Jamal, then Siffin and Nahrawan. Kumayl himself reports, "We were in Jamal and we were in a state of shock at how much hatred they had for our leader." This was a leader actually elected by the general population compared to predecessors, who were secretively selected by elite members of the community. Kumayl and his companions were dumbfounded by the hatred for the man who had so elegantly and eloquently brought Islam to Yemen.

Other schools in Islam discredit Kumayl ibn Ziyad because of his commitment to Imam Ali (as). For example, Ibn Habban notes, "His *hadiths* are weak because he had too much love for Ali ibn Abi Talib (as)." Whereas individuals such as Abdullah ibn Shaqiq, Khalid ibn Salama, Mehran al-Jizni, Abdullah ibn Salama, and Umar ibn Saad within the biographical texts are described as trustworthy *hadith* authorities, in spite of the appellation "hater of Ali ibn Abi Talib".

In Umar ibn Saad's biography one will find the additional description, "Trustworthy *tabi'i* of the generation after the Holy Prophet (pbuh). He killed Husayn (as), son of Ali (as), but his *hadiths* are all reliable."

Imam Ali (as), as soon as he became caliph, made Kumayl governor of Heet, which is an area in Iraq about 130 miles from Baghdad on the banks of the Furaat. It was a strategic area in relation to Shaam because of a river connecting the two lands. If left vulnerable, Muawiyah would not have hesitated to invade it. Thus, Kumayl was commanded not to leave his post.

Muawiyah wasted no time in creating a distraction that targeted an area called Kaffar Qus in Syria where another commander of Ali ibn Abi Talib (as), by the name of Shabath ibn Rabii, was under a lot of pressure. Kumayl promptly went to his aid against the command of Imam Ali (as) leaving Heet vulnerable, and in fact received the following letter from Imam Ali (as) when he later asked for permission to take revenge for the attack in Kaffar Qus:

It is wrong for a person to disregard and neglect the duty entrusted to him and try to take up the work entrusted to somebody else and at a time when he is not required to do it. Such an attitude indicates a weak and harmful mentality. Your desire to invade Kirkisiya and to leave your province undefended and unattended shows the confusion of your mind. By such an action you will convert yourself into a kind of bridge that your enemy can cross conveniently to reach your friends. Thus, you will be a useless auxiliary who has neither power, nor prestige, nor dignity, who cannot stop his enemy's in-roads, nor can crush him, and who cannot defend his subject nor can he be of any use or help to his ruler. (*Nahj al-Balaghah*, Letter 61)

There are times when a leader of any institution, however much he loves his deputies, must take measures to discipline them and guide them, particularly when tremendous pressure and deception is abound. Muawiyah was scheming through spies, infiltrators, disinformation, and attacks to destroy Imam Ali (as), and this move of Kumayl left him vulnerable. Fortunately, Kumayl returned back in time before Muawiyah captured his province.

Those were testing times for Ali ibn Abi Talib's (as) companions. They loved him and were devoted and obedient, but there were times when they doubted themselves and were unsure about their decisions.

Sometimes what seemed apparent was not always the truth, and this is where the wisdom of someone like Imam Ali (as) was superior. Imam Ali (as) invited Kumayl to take a walk with him sometime after the Battle of Siffin.

They walked past a house and heard a beautiful recital of the Qur'an issuing into the evening air. Kumayl was taken with this beautiful recital, and he wondered how religious and pious this fine reciter must be. Imam Ali (as) looked at Kumayl and said, "I will remind you of this man one day." Later, in the Battle of Nahrawan, Kumayl was fighting alongside Imam Ali (as) against the Khawarij, the very same soldiers who were once with Imam Ali (as) at Siffin, but now against him in Nahrawan.

When the battle was over, Kumayl and his compatriots had remained firm and none of their enemies had pierced them. The Imam (as) approached Kumayl and reminded him of the evening of their walk together. The Imam (as) showed him one of the slain opposition, and identified him as the reciter Kumayl had thought was so pious. Although his sound was so divine, his understanding was hollow; the man had fought the one whom the verses had praised.

Kumayl found that in the final days of the life of Ali ibn Abi Talib (as), the Imam began to reveal to him more of the secrets of this world, and amongst the most beautiful secrets was the Dua (supplication) of Khidhr.

One night in the mosque of Basra, Kumayl was sitting with a group where Imam Ali ibn Abi Talib (as) was giving a lecture about the importance of reciting the Dua of Khidhr, which he praised highly. He told them to recite the Dua of Khidhr on the 15th of Shaban, the Day of Arafah, or a Thursday night (once a week, a month, or a year). For the one who recited it, Allah (swt) would remove all evil and envy from him and provide sustenance.

Everyone went home after the lecture except Kumayl. He had questions about this amazing *dua* and was eager to learn more. Imam Ali (as) was willing to teach Kumayl because of his sincerity and his receptive heart.

Dua of Khidhr became known as Dua Kumayl and is a phenomenal supplication. It is one of those supplications that today's followers of the Ahl al-Bayt (as) actually look forward to reading week in and week out with each person finding a different line which they love. Some resonate with, "Oh Allah (swt), forgive those sins of mine that block my *dua* from being answered." Some are struck by the line, "I am willing to accept your punishment, but how can I bear separation from you?"

The line, "Who do I have other than you, oh Allah (swt)?" is a resonant truth that the devoted relish. Kumayl narrates another *dua*, but many forget it in spite of the eloquence expressed in this extraordinarily poetic and touching supplication. It is known as "Dua Sabah," and it is reads as a love poem to Allah (swt). For example:

Oh Allah, Oh He who extended the morning's tongue in the speech of its dawning, dispatched the fragments of the dark night into the gloom of its stammering, made firm the structure of the turning spheres in the measures of its display and beamed forth the brightness of the sun through the light of its blazing! Oh He, who demonstrates His Essence by His Essence, transcends comparison with His creatures and is exalted beyond conformity with His qualities!

The depth of spirituality in this *dua* is magnificent and gives one a glimpse into the radiance of his teacher, Imam Ali (as) and the spiritual capacity of the transmitter, Kumayl.

In the biography of Muhammad ibn Abu Bakr, his letter to Muawiyah revealed much about his character and his allegiance to Islam. Likewise, the following heart to heart exchange between Kumayl and Imam Ali (as) reveals the intimate trust between them. It is called the Hadith of Kumayl on Ilm (religious knowledge) and it describes the hearts of men and the merits of true religious knowledge. Kumayl narrates:

> Imam Ali (as) put his hand in my hand and took me to the desert quarter. When he travelled, he left the city behind. He heaved a sigh three times and said, 'Kumayl, these hearts are containers of the secrets of knowledge and wisdom, and the best container is the one that can hold the most of its contents and can preserve and protect them in the best way. Therefore,

remember carefully what I am telling you, oh
Kumayl. Remember, there are three kinds of people.
There are the people who are highly versed in the
ethics of truth and the philosophy of religion. The
second is the kind of people who are acquiring the
above knowledge. The third is that class of people
who are uneducated, but follow whatever is the trend.
They accept every slogan, they have neither acquired
knowledge nor have they secured any support of firm
and rational convictions.

Remember Kumayl, knowledge is better than wealth,
because it protects you, while you have to protect
wealth. Wealth decreases if you keep on spending it,
but the more you make use of knowledge, it increases.
But what you achieve through knowledge will remain
with you forever. Oh Kumayl, knowledge is power,
and it can command obedience. A man of
knowledge, during his lifetime can make people obey
and follow him, and he is praised and venerated after
his death. Remember, knowledge is a ruler, and
wealth is a subject.'

He left him with this wisdom and the distinguishing
characteristics of the three classes of human beings. He gave him the
gift of the greatest wealth that will never leave him and will never
diminish him.

Kumayl was privileged to have another exchange with the blessed Imam (as) and it is called the Hadith al-Haqiqah (the Reality, Ultimate Truth); and every spiritual school of Islam still discusses this area which is highly enigmatic. It was a gift to Kumayl and a privilege that the incredible Divine knowledge overflowing in the heart of Imam Ali (as) was spilled over into the heart of Kumayl, not merely because of his curiosity or probing, but because he was a worthy recipient. Kumayl reported the dialogue between them:

> I was riding a camel and Imam Ali (as) was in front of me. Then I looked at him and asked, 'What is the truth?' Imam Ali (as) turned around to me and said, 'What do you have to do with the truth?' I said, 'Aren't I the door to your secrets?' Imam Ali (as) said, 'What sprinkles in you, overflows in me.' Then the Imam (as) said, 'What is the truth? All of this. What is the truth? Who are you?' I then asked, 'Oh my master, am I not worthy to share in your secrets?' 'Yes,' answered Ali (as). 'But the matter is a great one.' 'Oh my master, do you desire that those who beg at the door of your bounty be turned away?' 'No,' answered Ali (as). 'Verily, I will answer the call of all who seek that which overflows in me, so they receive it from me according to their capacity.' Then the Imam (as) said, 'Kumayl, the truth is the revelation of the splendours of the divine Majesty

without a sign.' 'Oh my master,' I said, 'I understand not what you are meaning. Explain to me further.' Imam Ali (as) said, 'The defacement of the conjectured and the clearing of the known.' I said again, 'Explain to me more.' 'The rending of the veil by the triumph of mystery.' I asked again, 'Oh my beloved, tell me more.' He said, 'The attraction of the Divine Unity through the nature of the apprehension of its Divine Unicity.' I said, 'Tell me more.' He said, 'A light shining forth from the morning of eternity and irradiating the temples of the Unity.'

They continued riding their camel and Kumayl was left to ponder these deeply esoteric revelations uttered from a personality that was so devastatingly misunderstood by his enemies and barely appreciated by his followers. Truthfully, many mystics and scholars have studied this *hadith* and have hardly scratched the surface of its meanings, let alone lay people reading it for the first time.

Some scholars describe how the illumination mentioned here is only available to those who have truly shed egotistical views regarding God. The mystical scholars say that if one ever wanted to understand Ali ibn Abi Talib (as) as an axis between Allah and humanity, it was in these five lines.

When Imam Ali (as) died, Kumayl gave his oath of allegiance to Imam Hasan (as) and after Imam Hasan (as) died, Kumayl lived in the time of Imam Husayn (as). But there is an unanswered question, where was he during the tragedy of Karbala? Many learned people have been unable to answer this question, but it does seem clear that Kumayl was alive at the time of the events of Karbala and was around sixty to sixty-one years of age.

His contemporaries are accounted for; Mukhtar was in prison, Maytham, Hani ibn Urwa, and Muslim ibn Aqil were all killed, while Habib ibn Mudhahir made it to Karbala. An examination through other prominent contemporaries' biographies doesn't reveal his whereabouts. There is a Kumayl called Kumayl al-Hamadani, who was in prison with Mukhtar, but that is a different individual even though the Hamadanis were from Yemen as well.

So after Karbala, he seemingly comes back into the world of *hadith*, in about the eighty-first or eighty-second year after Hijrah. Twenty-one years after Karbala one hears the story of his execution. The caliph of the time was Abdul Malik ibn Marwan and his governor was Hajjaj ibn Yusuf al-Thaqafi, one of the cruellest and most heinous people in history. He is quoted as having said, "I wish I was alive on the tenth of Muharram, so I also could have beheaded Husayn (as)."

Hajjaj would recklessly jail people and forget about them. He would mockingly incite people to sacrifice anyone called Ali, Hasan, or Husayn on Eid al-Adha. It is reported that Hajjaj would even frequently refuse to eat bread until a soldier satisfied him by executing a Shī'ī Muslim and bring him their head. He would exclaim, "The bread tastes so much better," with the sight of their decapitated head.

One of his commanders was Abdul Rahman ibn Ash'ath, who led conquering troops to Persia, Iraq, and Turkey. Abdul Rahman wrote a letter to Hajjaj saying that their soldiers were losing morale and were tired in Turkey. Hajjaj wrote back to him saying, "Curse be on you and curse be on your soldiers. Don't be tired. Go and bring me victory. I don't have time for you being tired."

Abdul Rahman ibn Ash'ath, having heard that Hajjaj spoke like this about him after many previous incidents decided that it was time to rise against Hajjaj, but Abdul Malik ibn Marwan, in a move to avoid the uprising, had Hajjaj removed from power. The soldiers turned their anger against the Umayyads, who in turn reinstated Hajjaj. At this point Abdul Rahman continued his plan to pursue Hajjaj, and even though Kumayl was eighty-one years old he wanted to join the uprising against Umayyad injustice. Unfortunately, they did not find victory, but Kumayl managed to escape from the battle.

The pursuit for Kumayl ensued and in his stead, Hajjaj imprisoned Kumayl's wife and children and began torturing them. He made a public announcement about their arrest and taunted Kumayl that if he was truly a lover of Ali ibn Abi Talib (as), he should come out and defend his family. He came forward with his stick. Hajjaj taunted him even more, commanding him to disassociate from Imam Ali (as) and his opposition to the Umayyads. Kumayl replied, "Hajjaj, show me a way better. I will join that way.

But having searched this whole earth, I never found a way other than that of Ali ibn Abi Talib (as)."

Hajjaj ordered him prostrate on the ground and this man who had been a boy during the life of the Holy Prophet (pbuh) and an intimate friend of Imam Ali (as), was laid down and beheaded. His blood flowed across the streets of Kufa, until they went to bury him secretly near Masjid al-Kufa, in the area of Hanana. He was martyred at the age of eighty-three or eighty-four years. May Allah (swt) bless the soul of the keeper of Imam Ali's secrets and faithful companion of the Ahl al-Bayt (as), Kumayl ibn Ziyad.

Works Cited

Abi Talib, Ali. *Nahjul Balagha, Peak of Eloquence : Sermons, Letters, and Sayings of Imam Ali Ibn Abu Talib.* Ed. Mohammad Askari Jafery. (Elmhurst, NY: Tahrike Tarsile Quran, 1986).

Chapter 8:

Jabir ibn Abdullah

J abir ibn Abdullah al-Ansari occupies a prominent position in the religion of Islam as one of the greatest Companions of the Prophet Muhammad (pbuh), and the five Imams of the Ahl al-bayt (as). He knew and served every Imam, from Imam Ali (as) to Imam al-Baqir (as), whom he reportedly longed to meet since the time of the Holy Prophet (pbuh).

The Holy Prophet (pbuh) had prophesized that Jabir would one day have the blessing of meeting Imam al-Baqir (as). This Companion of the Noble Prophet (pbuh) carried his message through time to the future descendant of Allah's (swt) Messenger (pbuh). He is distinguished as one of the last to die amongst the Companions of the Holy Prophet (pbuh).

He had the precious honour of connecting many generations to the Holy Prophet (pbuh) through the teachings he directly received. Jabir was a man known for his valour, dedication, and knowledge. Few Companions in Islamic history come anywhere near the status of Jabir ibn Abdullah al-Ansari; he is revered for his conduct alongside the Prophet (pbuh) and his family (as).

Jabir ibn Abdullah al-Ansari had an honoured status with respect to the Ahl al-Bayt (as). This was a man whom the Holy Prophet (pbuh) selected and prophecized, "Oh Jabir, one day you will meet my great grandson Muhammad (as), who will be known as al-Baqir (as). Give him my greetings." For the Holy Prophet (pbuh) to have trusted an individual with such a portentous message meant that he was a man of sublime character.

Unfortunately, a comprehensive study on the life of Jabir ibn Abdullah al-Ansari does not exist in English. Even in the Arabic language, biographies on his life are few and far between. This brief biography gives one a glimpse of the blessed man who is credited with the first Ziyarah (visitation) of the burial place of Imam Husayn (as).

Jabir's full name was Jabir ibn Abdullah ibn Amr al-Ansari and he was born in the city of Medina. Any Companion of the Holy Prophet (pbuh) whose surname was Ansari meant that they were from the people of Medina. Their surname derived from the Arabic word *ansar,* meaning helpers who brought victory. The Meccan Companions who left Mecca to help the Prophet (pbuh) in Medina were called Muhajirun.

Those that helped the Holy Prophet's (pbuh) message in Medina were known as members of the Ansar. Jabir came from the richest family in Medina that owned a grand and expansive mansion next to Masjid Quba. Jabir's grandfather Amr, the father of Abdullah, was one of the wealthiest people in Medina. Jabir therefore was brought up in relative luxury.

Interestingly, one of the reasons the Holy Prophet (pbuh) migrated to Medina was because of Jabir's father. The Holy Prophet (pbuh) and his small community of followers suffered years of pressure, abuse, and hardship at the hands of the Quraysh and other ruling elite in the land of Mecca. They had left the Muslims no other option than to migrate to Medina after assassination attempts, forced exiles, economic sanctions, and years of torture.

The people of Medina knew of the qualities and noble character of the Holy Prophet (pbuh) and they were ripe for his message and for the blessings of a divine leader. The final year in Mecca, before the Holy Prophet (pbuh) migrated, a group from Medina came to him in the city of Mecca. The narrations mention that there were only twelve individuals who came to Mecca, where they famously pledged themselves to the Holy Prophet (pbuh) in an event known as the First Pledge of Aqabah.

They said, "Oh Prophet (pbuh) of God, we are the people of Medina. We have come to Mecca to tell you if the people of Mecca do not appreciate you, then know the people of Medina are waiting for you. If the people of Mecca do not appreciate the Qur'an, know the people of Medina are waiting for the Qur'an. If the people of Mecca do not appreciate your *akhlaq*, your morals, then the people of Medina await you. We have come here to pledge to you." The Holy Prophet (pbuh) told them to come back the following year and he would send an ambassador back with them to the land of Medina. After the year had passed, he sent one of his distant cousins, by the name of Musab ibn Umayr as ambassador to Medina.

Musab came from one of the richest families in Mecca and decadence was no stranger to him. Prior to embracing Islam, he was utterly indulged and spoiled as a child. If he desired a perfume from the land of Yemen, his mother would send a servant all the way there to endure a three-month journey for this perfume.

If he desired the most delectable and famous sweets of Syria, another servant would be dispatched with the sole purpose of securing these goods. Musab was a handsome and popular youth when he found the Holy Prophet (pbuh). After he began learning from the Prophet's noble character and exemplary leadership, he lost the taste for luxuries of this world. He was from amongst the earliest devotees that visited the Holy Prophet (pbuh) at the house of al-Arqam.

His own mother imprisoned him in his home after she discovered his movement towards Islam. He was eventually forced to part from his strong-willed mother who turned him out declaring she was no longer his mother while adamantly refusing to abandon her traditions. He even advised his mother, beseeching her that his heart was close to her, but she would not budge. Seeing this devotion to the religion and all the personal sacrifice of Musab, the Holy Prophet (pbuh) thought he was the best choice to become the ambassador to Medina.

Upon arriving in Medina, Musab met with the leading people there and elucidated the principles of the religion of Islam. He described the oneness of God, the Prophethood of Muhammad (pbuh), the worth and dignity of the human being, and the importance of keeping trusts, among other noble truths from the Holy revelation.

This meeting proved to be fruitful as he was an excellent orator and demonstrated a noble and reasonable character. The following year a bigger group of seventy-five individuals from Medina came to Mecca, two of them were women. Another contingent of three hundred Jews from Medina came as well.

There, they all pledged allegiance to the Holy Prophet (pbuh) in what is known as The Second Pledge of Aqabah where they agreed to listen and obey him at all times and in all situations, to share their resources in support of the religion, to enjoin the good and forbid the evil, to have complete trust in Allah (swt), and to defend the Holy Prophet (pbuh) in cases of war and aggression. Those who formally agreed and took the oath were told that Paradise would await them.

Now the young Muslim community could begin to find some sanctuary en masse to establish their beliefs and practices to reform society towards justice and God-consciousness. The new adherents from Medina came to the Holy Prophet (pbuh) and confirmed that they wanted him to join them in their city. In addition, they were hoping he would be able to bring peace and unity between the Banu Aws and the Banu Khazraj, two leading tribes in the city.

The Meccan Muslims, following the advice of the Holy Prophet (pbuh), slowly began moving to Medina in small groups. A first group of them went then another group led by Umar ibn Khattab migrated until there was a certain group left behind. Those were people like Ali ibn Abi Talib (as), Fatimah Zahra (as), Fatimah bint Asad - the mother of Imam Ali (as), Abu Bakr, and Fatimah bint Hamzah.

They were left behind until the Holy Prophet (pbuh) on the night of Hijrah told Ali ibn Abi Talib (as) to sleep on his bed as he was going to leave for Medina in the middle of the night. He told Ali (as) to bring the Fawatim with him, which is the plural of Fatimah, meaning Fatimah bint Asad - his mother, Fatimah bint Hamzah, his cousin, and Fatimah Zahra (as).

Amongst the men who told the Holy Prophet (pbuh) in both the first and second Pledge of Aqabah to come to Medina was Abdullah al-Ansari, the father of Jabir. Jabir's father Abdullah, pledge allegiance to the Holy Prophet (pbuh), declaring that he and his children were at his service. Abdullah al-Ansari had ten children, nine of which were girls and one boy, Jabir.

When the Holy Prophet (pbuh) established himself in Medina, Jabir would stick with the Holy Prophet (pbuh) wherever the Holy Prophet (pbuh) would go, whether he was in prayer, or walking around the city, Jabir would be behind him. There are *hadiths*, or narrations, that describe this close affection and affinity, "Every *salah*, Jabir would go from his house walking to Masjid al-Nabawi to pray behind the Holy Prophet (pbuh)." In Islam there are many traditions emphasizing the importance of attending group prayers at the mosques and to keep the mosques vibrant and active. For example, The Holy Prophet (pbuh) said:

> The rows of my followers in the congregational prayer on the earth are like the rows of angels in the sky; and a *rakah*, or unit, of prayer in congregation is equivalent to twenty-four *rakahs*, and every *rakah* with Allah, Almighty and Glorious, is more beloved than forty years of worship. Therefore, on the Day of Justice, when Allah gathers all human beings from the beginning to the end for Reckoning, there will be no believer who has attended the congregational prayer but for whom Allah will decrease the grievousness of the Day of Reckoning and after that the person will be told to enter Heaven.

The mosque is not just a venue for commemoration of the big events in the Islamic year, nor for the remembrance of just two Imams, but of all twelve and to remember them through implementing their devotional practices and services to humanity.

Jabir had the honour of knowing five of the imams. He respected and followed them all with the utmost commitment. He serves, therefore, as an extraordinary example for the followers of the Ahl al-Bayt (as) today to maintain a parallel devotion and connection. That devotion and connection is indeed part of a believer's obligation. In *Bihar al-Anwar* the following tradition states, "Surely, for every act of worship there is another superior to it, and love for the Ahl al-Bayt (as)--is the most superior act of worship."

Jabir had the privilege to sit under the pulpit of the Holy Prophet (pbuh) and he would take copious notes whenever the Holy Prophet (pbuh) spoke to the community. Those notes were compiled into what is known as the "Sahifah of Jabir ibn Abdullah al-Ansari", one of the greatest collections of *hadith* from the Holy Prophet (pbuh).

The freedom to worship, study Islam openly, to gather in public, and to implement Islamic ethics, are all indications that the Muslim community began to flourish when the Holy Prophet (pbuh) moved to Medina. However, plotting was still afoot amongst the archenemies of the Holy Prophet (pbuh). Abu Sufyan, Abu Lahab, Abu Jahl, Utbah ibn Rabi'a, and Walid ibn Mughirah would not rest agitating the community until they ended up attacking the Holy Prophet (pbuh) in the Battle of Badr.

Abdullah al-Ansari, Jabir's father, was fighting alongside the Holy Prophet (pbuh) at the Battle of Badr. Jabir who was in his late teens or early twenties, came to the battle ready to fight, but his father ordered him, "Get back! You are not ready to fight." His father wanted him to protect and look after his nine sisters, if his father was to die in that battle. Jabir, full of youthful passion and eagerness went pleading to the Holy Prophet (pbuh), begging him to allow him to fight. Jabir knew that *jihad* (defensive war against oppression) was *wajib*, obligatory, on the Muslim and he was more than ready to fight the opposition.

But the Holy Prophet (pbuh) reminded him that obedience to his father was also obligatory in Islam and he had been given the responsibility of the family should anything happen to his father. The Holy Prophet (pbuh) wanted to teach Muslims that fathers are everyone's roots in this world and that it is a Muslim's obligation to have reverence and give obedience to the father.

The Holy Prophet (pbuh) provided a compromise for the father and son. Jabir was instructed to serve Allah (swt) and the cause of the religion by to carrying water for the soldiers. This command of the Holy Prophet (pbuh) indicates that all acts, if done for the pleasure and service of Allah (swt) are acceptable, whether one is a man of the sword or a water carrier. Jabir faced the same censure from his father the following year at the Battle of Uhud, but on this occasion it was because of his father's concern for any debts he may have owed to others if he were to die in the battle. Abdullah al-Ansari had foresight knowing the risk he was undertaking and he didn't approach the battle without preparing his will, a *wasiyah*. He made sure Jabir was able to meet his obligations on his behalf.

Jabir ibn Abdullah al-Ansari again was giving out water at the next battle, the Battle of Uhud. He had the tragic misfortune to see his father killed next to Hamzah, the fierce warrior and uncle of the Holy Prophet (pbuh). As is well known in Islamic history Hind, the wife of Abu Sufyan and the mother of Muawiyah, ate the liver of

Hamzah and is called *akilat al-akbad* (the eater of livers) due to this heinous action. Of course such an act is not as simple as described, the poor victim's body had to also be ripped apart.

The Meccan women were even known to have cut off body parts and cut out organs of the bodies of the fallen soldiers to make trophy necklaces. These "Daughters of the Morning Star" as they called themselves in their diabolical chants during the battle, were dripping in the blood of the victims. There are certain books that say there was a second body that Hind desecrated as well, Abdullah al-Ansari, the father of Jabir.

Her hatred of Abdullah al-Ansari had to do with the fact that his wealth had supported the spread of the message of Muhammad (pbuh). Watching his father fighting without being able to come to his aid was already heart-wrenchingly difficult for Jabir. But Jabir was devastated seeing his beloved and virtuous father's body desecrated in such a brutal and evil way.

Another well-known fact about the battle of Uhud is that the soldiers fighting on the side of the Holy Prophet (pbuh) were told to hold their positions, but they abandoned them in a grab for the war booty. They ran from the hill which they were holding and thus exposed the Holy Prophet (pbuh) and his loyal Companions to a disastrous attack.

Abu Sufyan recognized that the moment presented him with his chance to kill Muhammad (pbuh). As Abu Sufyan was about to attack, the Holy Prophet (pbuh) called his remaining soldiers to aid him and to get the ready. At this precarious moment in Islamic history, Jabir answered the Prophet's call and joined the battle. When Abu Sufyan's army attacked, it is reported that he performed valiantly alongside Imam Ali (as). He was able to resist the attack and bring victory to the religion of Islam. Following this battle, Jabir fought alongside the Holy Prophet (pbuh) at Khandaq, Khaybar, and every subsequent battle.

Many of the most famous *hadith* are narrated by Jabir ibn Abdullah al-Ansari. For example, there is a *hadith* where Jabir said, "I heard the Holy Prophet (pbuh) say that for every disease, except for death, there is a cure and it is Surah al-Fatihah." He narrates from Fatimah Zahra (as) the Hadith al-Kisa, which is the narration describing the Holy Prophet (pbuh) gathering Fatimah Zahra (as), Imam Ali (as), Imam Hasan (as), and Imam Husayn (as) under his Yemeni cloak and proclaiming their purity with the revelation of the Verse of Purification (Q33:33). The report begins with the line, "Jabir ibn Abdullah al-Ansari narrates that he heard Fatimah Zahra (as) say..."

This famous *hadith* is transmitted by two more individuals as well, Umm Salma and Aisha, two of the wives of the Holy Prophet (pbuh). In another *hadith* from Jabir, he narrates that when the Twelfth Imam (as) returns, he will say to Prophet Isa (pbuh), "Oh Prophet of God (pbuh), you lead *salah*." Whereas Isa (pbuh) will reply to him, "No, *salah* was in your family. You are the one who has to lead *salat al-asr*." Likewise the *hadith* of al-Ghadir, "Of whomsoever I am his master, Ali (as) is also his master" is from Jabir ibn Abdullah al-Ansari.

The *hadith* about *mutah*, the temporary marriage (banned by Umar ibn Khattab) that was allowed by the Holy Prophet (pbuh) is narrated by Jabir ibn Abdullah al-Ansari. One of the biggest blessings in this religion is Allah (swt) lengthened the life of Jabir ibn Abdullah al-Ansari, so he could narrate the *hadith* from five Imams (as) of Aal Muhammad (as). He met all of them and was present to verify and confirm their *hadith* and those of their disciples.

Jabir had the privilege to support Ali ibn Abi Talib (as). After the Holy Prophet (pbuh) died, a few people at Saqifah selected the next leader after the Holy Prophet (pbuh) and ignored Imam Ali (as) despite the Prophet's appointment of him as their master. Only a few Companions remained loyal to Imam Ali (as), Abu Dhar, Salman, Ammar, Miqdad, Zubayr, Hudhayfah, and Jabir ibn Abdullah al-Ansari were among the few.

When people raided the house of Fatimah Zahra (as), Jabir was with Aal Muhammad (as). Jabir was at the funeral of Fatimah Zahra (as). In other words, at the most delicate stages of the succession to the Holy Prophet (pbuh), Jabir ibn Abdullah al-Ansari was always with Imam Ali (as). That's why Jabir didn't remain silent; when he had to speak out, he spoke out.

During the time when Imam Ali (as) was not caliph, Jabir stood in front of all of the Companions, knowing very well that they were present at the Day of Ghadir and told them that, "I am the one who saw the Holy Prophet (pbuh) lift the hand of Ali ibn Abi Talib (as), and say, 'Oh Ali (as), you and your partisans (Shi'a) will be the first to enter Paradise. Paradise awaits you.' The Holy Prophet (pbuh) said, 'Give glad tidings to your partisans, oh Ali (as), for when they die, we will raise them gently and judge them with justice and allow them to cross the bridge before others'."

Jabir would always repeat the merits of Ali ibn Abi Talib (as). He would not allow people to wash away the memory of the Imam (as). He remained loyal to Ali ibn Abi Talib (as) and was with him at the Battle of Jamal, Siffin, and Nahrawan.

Even after Imam Ali (as), he remained loyal to Imam Hasan (as). But he had a particular love and affection for Imam Husayn (as). One day, a man who came from Shaam entered Medina and began asking its residents, "Who is known for his generosity?" The people of Medina told him to ask Jabir ibn Abdullah al-Ansari since he was a Companion of the Holy Prophet (pbuh). Jabir replied to him, "The most generous man in Medina, and none comes near him, is Husayn son of Ali ibn Abi Talib (as)."

Jabir described how he saw Imam Husayn (as) showing generosity with money to people who let down his father Ali ibn Abi Talib (as). One example was Usama b. Zayd b. al-Haritha, the eighteen-year-old appointed by the Holy Prophet (pbuh) to lead an expedition. Companions had objected to Usama's age in the face of their presumed seniority. On the same grounds, there were some Muslims who objected to Imam Ali becoming caliph after the

Prophet's death. However, in both cases, the Prophet (pbuh) had explicitly approved of their authority and competency to command those older than them.

It is noted in history, that Usama once killed a man on the battlefield who said, "La ilaha illa Allah" (the testimony of faith), after the man had killed a Muslim. Usama killed him anyway because he considered such a conversion to have been false. A verse of the Qur'an (Q4:94) was revealed in criticism of Usama's conduct. The Prophet (pbuh) was so saddened and upset by his action, that Usama swore never to strike anyone who uttered that statement again. Thus, when the civil wars began during the caliphate of Imam Ali (as), Usama asked him permission to abstain from the Battles of Jamal, Siffin, and Nahrawan. Usama did not want to be involved in any wars that required fighting other Muslims. Since Usama had made his oath in the presence of the Holy Prophet (pbuh), there is some indication that the Ahl al-bayt (as) accepted his excuse (*Rijal al-Kashi*, 1:192-199).

As Usama was approaching death, he had an outstanding loan, which was in the range of sixty thousand dinars. Usama turned to the family of the Holy Prophet (pbuh) for help. He came to Imam Husayn (as) and begged him for help.

This is the family of generosity, the family about which Surah al-Insan and Surah al-Dhar were revealed; thus Imam Husayn (as) paid the loan. People came to ask the Imam (pbuh) why he helped someone who abandoned his father, and the Imam (as) replied that it is the character of a Muslim to help those in need, for Allah (swt) will judge between the two on the Day of Judgment. Furthermore, such generosity can be soul changing for people as it was for Usama.

That is why Imam al-Baqir (as) says, "May Allah (swt) have mercy on Usama, Usama asked for forgiveness from Allah (swt), so do not speak ill of him." At least Usama asked for forgiveness, there were others who were so arrogant that before they died, they sought no forgiveness from Allah (swt) for refusing to help Ali ibn Talib (as), showing animosity towards him, or even going to war against him.

At the conclusion of the Battle of Nahrawan there were soldiers of the opposition who were caught, and one of these soldiers looked at Imam Husayn (as) and pleaded with him to ask his father Imam Ali (as) to have the rope that was binding him loosened for it was hurting him. It was the standard of the commander, Imam Ali (as), to always insist that the ropes binding the captured soldier's hands not hurt them.

That is why Rumi used to say about Imam Ali (as), "In bravery, you are the lion of your Lord, but in generosity, who knows who you are." So Imam Husayn (as) loosened the ties about his hands for him. That man asking for this leniency and sympathy was none other than the cruellest and most savage killer Shimr ibn Dhil Jawshan who beheaded Imam Husayn (as) in Karbala a few years later.

Due to his advanced age, Jabir was blind like Ibn Abbas around the time of Karbala. Some of the narrations mention that he was seventy-two years of age, and so consequently he could not accompany Imam Husayn (as) to Karbala. Later he heard about what happened at Karbala, how Shimr sat on the chest of Husayn (as) to decapitate him. He was devastated when he heard about the killer of Imam Husayn (as) repaying the leniency and generosity of the Ahl al-Bayt (as) with such horror.

He lived for seventeen years after Karbala and the narrations mention that he would sit outside the mosque of the Holy Prophet (pbuh) and he would say, "Where is al-Baqir (as)? Where is Muhammad (as)? Where is Muhammad (as)? Where is al-Baqir (as)?" The people would walk past and think he was crazy and that old age had gotten to him; they would make fun of him and the children would laugh at him. He would repeat this call because he remembered what the Holy Prophet (pbuh) had promised him.

Finally, one day he heard footsteps and he said, "Those are like the footsteps of the Holy Prophet (pbuh). Who is that?" The reply came that it was Muhammad, son of Ali (as), al-Baqir al-Ulum, the one who digs knowledge from the roots, the splitter of knowledge. He embraced him and began to cry. Those present asked him why he was crying. He said:

"The Holy Prophet (pbuh) said to me 'Oh Jabir, after me it will be Ali ibn Abi Talib (as) who will be the leader of the Muslims, then Hasan ibn Ali (as), then Husayn (as), then Zayn al-Abidin (as). Then after him will be Muhammad who is known as Baqir al-Ulum (as). O Jabir, send my *salam* (greetings of peace) to

Imam al-Baqir (as).'" Jabir said, "I have now fulfilled the *salam* of your great-grandfather the Holy Prophet (pbuh). I have now brought the *amanah*, the trust, forward and I have given you that *amanah*." He was honoured and Jabir went on to tell him, "Your grandfather the Holy Prophet (pbuh) would always say to me, 'After Imam Husayn (as), how can we prove Imamah?'"

One of the proofs of the Imamate of Imam al-Baqir (as) is the prophecy that Jabir would meet him. Whereas the Hadith al-Kisa is a proof for the Imams up until Imam Husayn (as), Jabir met Imam Zayn al-Abidin (as) and Imam al-Baqir (as) as prophesized by the Holy Prophet (pbuh).

There was a great honour for Jabir ibn Abdullah al-Ansari after he died. The King of Iraq around the 1930's, King Faysal, had an advisor by the name of Nuri Pasha who said that in a dream, "I saw Jabir ibn Abdullah al-Ansari three times, one night after another. I saw him saying to me 'My grave is being flooded over by the Tigris. Please help me.' I woke up and went to King Faysal telling him about Jabir's grave in the dream."

The king was astonished and reported that he had seen the same dream; together they went to the grave of Jabir. They brought a group of German specialists who were present at this major event. One of the Germans saw the body of Jabir from the grave looking as if he had recently passed away. He was so astonished from this experience that he converted to the religion of Islam. They also rebuilt the grave that indeed had become flooded. The grave of Jabir can be visited today in the land of Iraq. His grave is next to Hudhayfah's grave.

Jabir ibn Abdullah al-Ansari is also honoured through the blessing of having descendants that reflect his noble character. The great scholar of the religion of Islam, Sheikh Murtadha al-Ansari is from the descendants of Jabir ibn Abdullah al-Ansari. This eminent scholar is the author of a large number of books that make up the main curriculum of the *hawzah* (Islamic seminary). But one of the most amazing and most famous legacies of Jabir ibn Abdullah al-Ansari was that he performed the first Ziyarah (visitation) of the grave of Imam Husayn (as).

Specifically, the followers of the Ahl al-Bayt (as) have the *dua* of Visitation from Jabir entitled the "Ziyarah al-Arbaeen of Imam Husayn (as)." This supplication commemorates the fortieth day following the death of Imam Husayn (as). The initiative for this pilgrimage began when the blind Jabir was in Medina. Ibn Ziyad sent Abdul Malik al-Salami to the people of Medina to announce the murder of Imam Husayn (as).

When Jabir found out, he came to his servant Attiyah. Attiyah, who had received his name from Imam Ali (as), was one of the scholars of Aal Muhammad (as). He was a man who narrated the sermon of Sayedah Fatimah (as) regarding the land of Fadak. Jabir said to him, "Take me to Karbala."

Jabir reached Karbala on the fortieth day after the death of Imam Husayn (as). When he reached there, he performed acts that have become symbolic and devotional acts for others to emulate when performing the Ziyarah of Imam Husayn (as). The first thing he did was he took his shoes off and walked barefoot on the land of Karbala. He couldn't bring himself to walk to the grave of Imam Husayn (as) in comfort and with his shoes.

He thought of the pain that Imam Zayn al-Abidin (as), Zaynab and all of the relatives of Imam Husayn (as) endured under the oppressive soldiers of Yazid. He then went to the Furaat, the Euphrates, and performed another devotional act: the *ghusl*. He washed himself with the blessed water of the Euphrates, water that never reached the mouth of Imam Husayn (as). After that, he walked towards the grave of Imam Husayn (as) and he called out three times, "God is great. God is great. God is great. Oh Husayn (as). Oh Husayn (as). Oh Husayn (as)." The narrations mention that as soon as he got to the grave, he faced the grave where Imam (as) was buried and he said, "Oh Husayn (as), Oh Husayn (as), Oh Husayn (as)." But he didn't hear a reply.

The blind Jabir didn't hear a reply and he heart-wrenchingly called out, "Is this the way the lover answers his beloved?" He fell on the grave of Imam Husayn (as) and rubbed his cheeks on the dust and the grave of Imam Husayn (as).

There is a *hadith* from Imam al-Sadiq (as) that says, "Oh Allah (swt), have mercy on those cheeks that rub themselves on the grave of Imam Husayn (as)." Then his servant Attiyah called to Jabir warning him that he saw people coming from far away. Jabir replied that if it was the army of Ibn Ziyad, they should go, but if it was his master Imam Zayn al-Abidin (as), then they should stay. It was indeed the Imam (as) and he had come to complete the burial.

The narrations mention that Imam Zayn al-Abidin (as) had the head of Imam Husayn (as) and as he prepared to bury the head with the body, a call issued from the grave, "The baby! The baby! Place him on my chest." Imam Zayn al-Abidin (as) gently laid the six-month old baby on the chest of Imam Husayn (as) and then buried the head with the body. Jabir now came close to the Imam (as) and pleaded with him to tell him what happened to his beloved father Imam Husayn (as) on the plains of Karbala.

The grieving Imam (as) began to tell him, "Oh Jabir, where do you want me to begin narrating about what happened at Karbala? Oh Jabir, do you want me to tell you about my uncle Abbas, when he lay on the ground without his hands? Oh Jabir, do you want me to tell you about Rabab when she saw the baby on the ground with the arrow piercing his neck? Oh Jabir, do you want me to tell you when I saw Shimr sitting on the chest of my father and I saw the dagger cutting his neck?"

Jabir wept at the tragedy that he pictured, remembering how he had seen the generosity of Imam Husayn (as) and all the years he struggled alongside the blessed family of the Holy Prophet (pbuh). He wept at the injustice of those usurpers who violently removed from the earth the divine gifts to humanity who offered salvation to all. Jabir had a love for Imam Husayn (as) and all the Ahl al-Bayt (as) that was exceptional.

Works Cited

Al-Shaykh Muḥammad al-Ṭūsī. *Ikhtiyār maʿrifat al-rijāl, al-maʿrūf bi-rijāl al-Kashshī.* (Qum: 1983), vol. 1:205-240 (for the entry on Jābir).

Chapter 9:

Miqdad ibn al-Aswad

Miqdad ibn al-Aswad occupies a prominent position in Islamic history as one of the greatest Companions, not only of the Holy Prophet (pbuh) but also of Imam Ali (as). He is a man who displayed great valour, passion, and commitment for the religion of Islam throughout his life. Miqdad also demonstrated leadership skills that were exemplary and worthy of emulation.

Reports often mentioned his name alongside those of Salman, Abu Dhar, and Ammar. In a famous narration from the Holy Prophet (pbuh), he states, "Allah has ordered me to love four; he has ordered me to love Abu Dhar, Salman, Ammar, and Miqdad." Many in the Muslim community have asked, "Why is it that Miqdad deserves that love?" Within Shi'a communities today, many know the stories of these three personalities, but do not know anything about the life of Miqdad.

If one were to ask Muslims today, "What impact did Miqdad have on early Islamic history?" One would find Muslims unable to answer despite having heard his name in numerous lectures and *hadith*.

Regrettably, the community remains unaware of why Miqdad is so deserving of praise. Indeed, it is vital to study his biography in order to appreciate his contributions and understand key events within the early and decisive period of Islam. Whereas there are numerous significant events during the holy month of Ramadan that are well known and commemorated, such as Laylat al-Qadr (The Night of Power), the death anniversary of Sayedah Khadijah (as), the birth anniversary of the second Imam, Hasan al-Mujtaba (as), and the martyrdom of Imam Ali (as), the night of the 17th of Ramadan is overlooked.

On that night, Islam achieved its first victory in the battle of Badr, a significant occasion worthy of reverence during the holy month. The battle of Badr brought pride to the religion of Islam in its earliest and most sensitive days. Miqdad had a major role to play in that battle, as well as a major role to play in the lives of the Holy Prophet (pbuh) and Imam Ali (as).

An analysis of life of Miqdad through the lenses of Shi'ism is also an opportunity to demonstrate that the followers of the Ahl al-Bayt (as) indeed venerate many Companions of the Prophet (pbuh). It would be false to characterize Imamis as possessing enmity for the Companions of the Holy Prophet (pbuh) and excessive love for the Household. Both Sunni and Shi'i literature highly revere certain Companions of the Holy Prophet (pbuh) in their respective traditions. In each school, there are certain individuals who are prominent for their unwavering loyalty, bravery, commitment and steadfastness.

Companions came from different tribes, races, economic statuses, and positions, but found the call to Islamic fraternity and the divine religion an irresistible desire. While they may have come from illustrious or inglorious pasts, what makes certain Companions revered in Shī'ism is their immovable and resolute commitment to the religion of Islam, the Holy Prophet (pbuh), and his Household (as). Companions of this caliber moved from lower to higher states of spiritual nobility and along this wayfaring path, they never lost their way nor lagged behind.

The criteria for them to occupy a lofty position within the Islamic community was not simply their physical presence at the time of the Holy Prophet (pbuh) nor the fact that they may have once been worthy of praise and pious, but that their movement was spiritually upward bound. The Holy Qur'an itself confirms that mere proximity to the Holy Prophet is not the means to gain status or a lofty rank in the eyes of Allah (SWT). In Surah al-Tawbah, The Repentance, there is reference after reference to the hypocrites. Verse 101 in particular points out that Allah (swt) is aware of those who are sincere and those who are hypocrites surrounding the holy personality of Muhammad (pbuh):

"Of the desert Arabs round about you are hypocrites, as well as among the Medina folk: they are obstinate in hypocrisy. Thou knowest them not: We know them: twice shall We punish them:

and in addition shall they be sent to a grievous penalty"
(Q9:101).

Nonetheless, one must have an appreciation for the ardent
connection that Sunnism maintains with the Companions of the
Holy Prophet (pbuh). This love for them may have emerged out of a
longing to be one of the blessed individuals who sat in the company
of the Holy Prophet (pbuh). To have sat in the light cast from his
luminous personality, to have drunk from his well of divine
knowledge and imminent spirit, to have been elevated spiritually by
his mere presence is an unfathomable honour.

The projection of one's self into the role of a Companion will
lead to greater appreciation for their legacy and sacrifice. However,
one should not allow this love for Companions to cross beyond the
bounds of their actual deeds. The goal here is to go beyond mere
physical presence and proximity to the Holy Prophet, and examine
Companions with a more discerning eye. As a result, certain
Companions such as Miqdad will receive the due and value they
deserve.

Miqdad was born in the year 586 CE and was sixteen years
younger than the Holy Prophet (pbuh). His name appears in some
books as Miqdad ibn Amr al-Bahrai, whereas in other books he is
called Miqdad ibn al-Aswad ibn Abu Yaghut Zuhri. His biological
father was Amr al-Bahrai, a resident of the outskirts of Mecca and a
wealthy landowner with tracts spanning from Egypt to Sudan to

Ethiopia. As was common in the pre-Islamic period, emotion and passions reigned and the rule of law and civil society were unknown. Miqdad's father and his tribe were notorious for their volatile and vengeful behaviour. It wasn't uncommon for small disagreements or irritations to escalate into murder. The Holy Qur'an describes these types of people who lived without civil society and without rule of law.

Two similar words are used, Arab and *aaraab*. Arab means an Arabian, however *aaraab* means a Bedouin who has no law. Many of these Arabs of this time period were also *aaraab*, meaning Bedouins without a legal system. Vindictive and aggressive reactions abounded and a legal system was not established. It wasn't until the advent of Islam and the leadership of the Holy Prophet (pbuh) that this lawlessness was checked. The extent in which he was able to transform his society is quite remarkable. He established a legal system that sought to protect the property, honour, intellect, life and religion of human beings.

But prior to this legal system, Miqdad's father, Amr al-Bahrai, killed someone who had aggravated him. He was then exiled from Mecca and forced to go to Yemen. Once there, he married Miqdad's mother and thereafter, Miqdad was born. It is no surprise that Miqdad came out like his father's family, but his mother's family was equally infamous.

Members of his mother's tribe were notorious as gangsters who would easily murder and destroy others for any perceived threat to their power or control. It is reported that Miqdad used to say, "When I was younger, my uncles would place me near a tree and each one of them with their bow and arrow, would try and shoot an arrow that would just miss my eye." Miqdad followed suit; he grew into an equally aggressive and criminal young man, who acted without forethought. For example, the narrations state that one day there was a person by the name of Shimr ibn Hajar al-Kindi who aggravated him and Miqdad stabbed him.

The news of this act reached the tribe of Miqdad's mother, and along with it, the threats of escalating retaliation by Shimr ibn Hajar al-Kindi. Miqdad's maternal tribe attempted to assuage Shimr and his kinsmen by reminding them of Miqdad's connections to a renowned tribe in Yemen, this being one of the only recourses to staving off conflict in the pre-Islamic period.

Miqdad's maternal tribe had attempted to establish dominance and superiority through kinship and tribal alliances. Regardless of this attempt, Shimr's tribe was unrelenting and would not agree to leave Miqdad untouched and free. The only other option was for him to escape and leave his homeland. His mother advised him to go to Mecca and endeavour to align himself with a welcoming tribe.

He followed this advice and travelled the long and arduous journey to Mecca. Once there, he was able to align himself with the

Banu Zuhrah whose leader was a man by the name of al-Aswad. It was the custom in Arabia that when another tribe adopted someone, the head of the tribe's name would be given to that person. Hence in some books of *hadith*, one will find him referred to as Miqdad ibn al-Aswad, or by his birth father's original name, Amr al-Bahrai.

Miqdad joined the Banu Zuhrah tribe during the very early period of Islam when tribal leaders were fiercely opposed to the Holy Prophet (pbuh), attacking him from every angle both verbally and physically. The pressure upon Muhammad (pbuh) was unrelenting; the power structure of Mecca did not want to relinquish its position and age-old traditions.

The chief of the Banu Zuhrah tribe, al-Aswad ibn Abu Yaghut al-Zuhri, was known as one of the archenemies of the Holy Prophet (pbuh). In fact, a verse from the Holy Qur'an was revealed about Miqdad's adopted father, al-Aswad, and four other personalities: "For sufficient are We unto thee against those who scoff" (Q15:95).

The first of the four individuals was a man by the name of Walid ibn Mughirah, the father of Khalid ibn Walid. The narrations reveal that this Walid ibn Mughirah was known to be extremely arrogant, for example he would be enflamed with rage upon hearing the eloquent Arabic of the Qur'an. He knew that the Arabic of the Qur'an was more powerful than his own Arabic, and at this time verbal prowess and poetry was a sign of strength and position.

Clearly this eloquent Qur'anic Arabic would out do him and he would lose his prestige. As a consequence he began to make fun of the Holy Prophet (pbuh). Not only would Walid ibn Mughirah constantly ridicule the Holy Prophet (pbuh), but also when he would see the Holy Prophet (pbuh) in his prayers, he would throw the feces of an animal on his back. In addition to this public humiliation and degradation, he would intimidate the early Muslims by torturing some from among them.

But Allah (swt) is just and the only one to whom all pride belongs, so this Walid ibn Mughirah met his fate as a consequence of his very own arrogance. On his way home from work one day, he passed by a blacksmith shop and a splinter lodged itself into his ankle. Despite the pain and the potential for infection, he was unwilling to bend low in front of the tribal locals to remove it.

This same unwillingness to physically bow down was one of the main reasons some of the Arabs refused to embrace Islam, despite agreeing with other aspects of the religion such as treating neighbours fairly, looking after the poor, and being just to the orphans. When the Holy Prophet (pbuh) described the ritual prayers to them, specifically the prostration of the head on the ground, they adamantly refused to place their heads lower than their backsides nor upon the earth in humility.

Thus, Walid went home unwilling to bend low to remove the splinter. When he arrived home, his servant was cleaning his chamber and again he refused to bend low in front of another individual; at this point he decided to sleep and remove it later. The next day he did not awake.

The second person referred to in the verse mentioned above is al-Aas ibn Wa'il, the father of Amr ibn al-Aas. Al-Aas used to make fun of the Holy Prophet (pbuh) after his sons died, taunting him that he had no posterity to look after his message. He would further insult him by saying that his lineage was *abtar* (cut off). This was a serious insult in a period of patriarchy, when the wealth of having sons who would exclusively carry the family name, power, and status was of great import.

The Arabs of the pre-Islamic era considered it an honour to have sons, and by contrast a disgrace to have daughters. Ali Shariati describes this dichotomy in his book, *Fatima is Fatima*:

> Arab tribal society gave all the human values to a son, whereas a daughter was considered to lack all virtues and human authenticity....A boy had the material power to generate capital, aid society, and perpetuate the patriarchal system. He had prestige, fame, value, and spiritual credit. He supported the authenticity of the family. He was the giver of security and subsistence and the future authority of the family. But a girl was nothing. She was considered to be so weak that she must always be protected. (152-153)

So on many occasions that the Holy Prophet (pbuh) would walk the streets, al-Aas would verbally assault him saying, "*Abtar, abtar.* Your line is cut, your line is cut." Ironically, there is some question as to his own parentage[3] and his taunts take on a sharp irony. Nonetheless, the reply to these insults came directly from the Holy Revelation when Allah (swt) said, "For he who hateth thee, he will be cut off" (Q108:3). Al-Aas ibn Wa'il is the one to whom the Qur'an condemns, and by contrast, affirms that abundance is indeed the inheritance of Muhammad (pbuh), "To thee have We granted the Fount [of Abundance]" whereby his progeny would come from his beloved and honorable daughter, Fatimah al-Zahra (as).

Shariati notes that the word, *kawthar* or fount of abundance, means fullness, progeny, and blessings (Shariati, 153). Herein lies another revolutionary way in which the Holy Prophet transformed his society: in the case of Fatima, he elevated the status of the female as the source of lineage and authenticity of the family.

The third individual to have been amongst the scoffers was a man by the name of Haarith ibn Tulatala, and the fourth one was the adopted father of Miqdad al-Aswad. Regardless of al-Aswad's unending taunts of the Holy Prophet (pbuh), he never replied in kind but remained dignified, benevolent, and humble. This made a

---

[3] In the sermons of Imam Ali called the *Nahj al-Balaghah*, Amr ibn al-Aas is referred to by his mother's name, an-Nabigha, because his mother is reported to have been not only with al-Aas ibn Wa'il, to whom parentage has been attributed, but with four other men, thus putting into question whether al-Aas indeed had a known lineage at all.

deep impression on Miqdad who was raised to retaliate ferociously with double the taunts and threats.

He had never witnessed such tranquility of spirit, such unflinching demeanour, such strength of self-control; observing the calm of the Prophet touched him to the core. It was the key to unlocking his heart toward the religion of Islam.

Some *hadith* mention that Miqdad was the seventh convert to the religion of Islam. A question is often raised however regarding the time period of his conversion since the historical accounts only mention his aid to the Holy Prophet (pbuh) in Medina, not in Mecca. The reply is that the Holy Prophet (pbuh) advised him to keep his conversion to Islam silent as long as he was a client to a Meccan tribe. He was advised to dissimulate his faith, or perform *taqiyyah*.

One can only imagine how difficult it was for Miqdad to restrain himself when he used to see the early converts such as Ammar being tortured. He saw the Muslims flee to Abyssinia for refuge. But he waited for that day when he would join the religion openly and allow himself to be alongside the Holy Prophet (pbuh).

That day came when Abu Sufyan began his attacks on Medina. When the Holy Prophet (pbuh) moved to Medina, Abu Sufyan was angered by his success there. Despite Abu Sufyan's failed efforts to kill Muhammad (pbuh) and to trample his message, he continued to plot.

Abu Sufyan rallied the people of Mecca to fight against Muhammad (pbuh) and his followers by rumour-mongering. He sent a rumour back to Mecca that his trading caravan had been struck, and all of the Arab's wealth that had come from abroad had now been seized by Muhammad (pbuh) and his army. This rumour had no validity whatsoever, but the powerful figures of Mecca, such as Abu Jahl, Abu Lahab, Umayyah ibn Khalaf, Utbah ibn Rabi'ah, and Walid ibn Mughirah, would be easily moved to attack when they believed their wealth to have been plundered and pillaged.

Abu Sufyan took two hundred people with him to the outskirts of Medina, and amongst them was Miqdad. Miqdad chose this opportunity to join him as it was a means of reaching the Prophet (pbuh) himself. He planned to escape from Abu Sufyan's troops once the attack was underway. Miqdad went to Abu Sufyan with the request to join him; then with a man by the name of Utbah ibn Ghazwan they reached the outskirts of Medina.

When the skirmish took place, Abu Sufyan had two hundred soldiers with him and those fighting on behalf of the Holy Prophet (pbuh) numbered sixty, although he was not present himself. By the time Abu Sufyan returned with his soldiers he had only one hundred ninety-eight individuals with him; he began to question his fighters as to where the other two had gone. They reported that the two had been seen running towards the side of Muhammad (pbuh), calling out "*La Illaha Illallah, Muhammadan Rasoolallah*", "There is no god but the God, and Muhammad is his Messenger."

The two were Miqdad and Utbah ibn Ghazwan. When Miqdad reached the Holy Prophet (pbuh), Miqdad embraced him with fervour and devotion. All those years Miqdad had held back and could not admit that he was a Muslim; had been a challenging test of patience. Once in Medina he was able to openly support the Holy Prophet (pbuh).

The narrations tell us Miqdad used to say, "Those early days in Medina were the best days." He reports that for every *Ansari* (local Medinese Muslim) there were ten *Muhajirun* (Emigrants from Mecca) staying as guests in his home. Miqdad received incredible hospitality as the Holy Prophet (pbuh) himself wanted Miqdad to stay in his blessed house. What a status and what love the Prophet gave Miqdad, while all other Companions stayed in other homes, Miqdad stayed with him.

Miqdad himself narrates that one night when he was in the house of the Holy Prophet (pbuh) there was some milk available that he wanted to drink, and even though the Prophet (pbuh) had not yet had any, he took some for himself, however small the amount. He thought there would be more milk available for the Holy Prophet (pbuh).

Miqdad then felt remorse that Satan had tempted him to drink; he went to the Holy Prophet (pbuh) and begged his forgiveness for drinking before him and more importantly, for not even asking him. The Holy Prophet (pbuh) made a beautiful and generous supplication in response, "Ya Allah, quench the thirst of Miqdad for the rest of his life." Imagine the generosity and compassion of Muhammad (pbuh) as a gracious host.

The Holy Prophet (pbuh) had seen this young man Miqdad come from a strong tribal family, where he had once enjoyed comfort and clout. Miqdad could have easily rejected Islam out of arrogance. However, his patience and devotion to the Holy Prophet (pbuh) was stronger than any other temptation.

Abu Sufyan began his rumour mongering that led to the Battle of Badr. As his troops mobilised, Abu Sufyan saw this Miqdad at the centre of the army of the Holy Prophet (pbuh). He observed Miqdad's commitment with venom.

After a small skirmish, Abu Sufyan sent his messenger to Mecca and Abu Jahl heard the rumour of the pillaged caravan. The news enraged him and he immediately called for the biggest army to be prepared to fight Muhammad (pbuh). An army was assembled with nine hundred and fifty soldiers and the best of horses and camels with the intention to destroy Muhammad's (pbuh) fledging community. The arrogance and confidence that Abu Jahal displayed in this show of combativeness made clear that he did not understand the type of leadership that the Holy Prophet (pbuh) had with him.

When the Holy Prophet (pbuh) became aware of Abu Sufyan's rumours and Abu Jahl's army of nine hundred fifty, the narrations say that the Holy Prophet (pbuh) came to the Ansar, the Helpers, and Muhajirun, the Emigrants, calling upon their help.

He asked the head of the Ansar, whose name was Sa'd, if he was ready to help him. Sa'd most willingly agreed stating that even if the Holy Prophet (pbuh) asked him and his soldiers to plunge their horses into the seas in order to defend him, they and their horses were ready for the Holy Prophet (pbuh). All of the Ansar, two hundred and thirty three of them, were ready and willing to help. The Muhajirun, who were headed by the Holy Prophet (pbuh), were asked as well if they were willing to help. One Companion came forward and expressed doubt whether they had the strength to fight the Meccans since the opposition was very strong. Another Companion stated that they were no match for the Meccans' numbers since their army was made up of only three hundred thirteen soldiers. This was a decisive moment and Miqdad refuted both of them stating:

> Oh Holy Prophet (pbuh), we will not tell you what
> the Children of Israel told Moses. 'Go you to your
> Lord and we will stay behind.' Oh Holy Prophet
> (pbuh), if you ordered us to travel with you to the
> outer regions of Yemen, we will be on your left, and
> on your right, and in the front, and behind. Oh Holy

Prophet (pbuh), our lives are ready to be sacrificed for you.

That stand of Miqdad rallied the soldiers and bolstered their courage and zeal to the highest levels. He became a leader in that battle within the ranks of the Holy Prophet (pbuh). He decisively stepped forward with commitment and solidified his loyalty to Muhammad and the religion of Islam denouncing the cowardly stand of those who allowed fear to overtake them. He wouldn't tell the Holy Prophet (pbuh) what the Children of Israel said to Moses, "Go you to your Lord. We will stay here in safety." His example inspired the other soldiers and he ensured their unity and resolve. It was because of his galvanizing force that the day of Badr truly belonged to Miqdad.

That day without doubt, belonged decidedly to Imam Ali (as) as well. From the seventy who were killed in the opposition, thirty-five were from the sword of Ali ibn Abi Talib (as) alone. One narration states that Ali ibn Abi Talib (as), when he came out on the battlefield that day said, "I am like a raging spirit possessed, for a day like this, my mother gave birth to me..."

Imam Ali's (as) stance of courage and strength was indomitable; no one from the opposition stood a chance in front of him. The first stroke of death Imam Ali (as) inflicted was a pivotal stroke that shaped the future of Islamic history. Utbah ibn Rabi'ah, Muawiyah's maternal grandfather, was the recipient of that deadly blow in that significant encounter.

This event is commemorated at Siffin, when Imam Ali (as) challenges Muawiyah to fight him one to one, telling him that he will finish him with one stroke just as he did his maternal grandfather. He addresses him to come out as his forefather did and he will meet him just as he did the former. Furthermore, Imam Ali (as) advances the challenge to his sons and future generations, one after another.

At the Battle of Badr, Imam Ali (as) was the centre of swordsmanship and fighting skill, without question the right hand of the Holy Prophet (pbuh). Miqdad was the centre of the motivational energy and courageous leadership of that movement. But this pair not only stood unshakably with the Holy Prophet (pbuh) at Badr, but also were definitive leaders at Uhud.

If it weren't for Miqdad, Imam Ali (as), and a courageous lady, the Holy Prophet (pbuh) would have been alone on the mountain of Uhud. The audacity, greed, and disobedience of many were revealed that day when the seal of Prophets and the divinely appointed guide was left practically alone on a battlefield.

The narrations state that Holy Prophet (pbuh) warned the soldiers, "Oh my dear soldiers, beware, do not leave me alone on the mountain because Khalid ibn Walid is planning to come around the side of the mountain, and if he comes around the side, he will attack me." These soldiers saw that the Muslims had virtually destroyed the opposition and that others from amongst them were immediately picking up the spoils of war, the shields, the swords, and other trinkets that remained on the fallen soldiers.

Those who were warned not to abandon, decided for themselves that the victory was decisive and the battle was over. They left the Holy Prophet (pbuh) alone, undefended and ran towards the battlefield for the glittering things of this world. The Holy Prophet (pbuh) was stranded alone with the opposition charging towards him from the rear. He fought them, with Imam Ali (as) on one side and Miqdad on the other.

It can easily be said that these three fighting at this critical moment were literally fighting to save the religion. Miqdad became close to Imam Ali (as) after this momentous and precarious event because he was drawn to the latter's valour.

Not only was his valour remarkable, but his age; Imam Ali (as) was twenty-five at the battle of Uhud. During the prime of his life he was getting showered with arrow after arrow and receiving wound after wound. Fatimah al-Zahra (as) treated sixty-three wounds on the body of Ali ibn Abi Talib (as) at the Battle of Uhud. Miqdad, who was fourteen years his senior, looked at Imam Ali (as) and was awestruck by how this undaunted twenty-five year old was saving Islam from peril.

Whereas today one may find many in the community who can barely commit to the ritual prayers, observing Islamic dress, or even becoming acquainted with the Holy text of the Qur'an, this story of valour and commitment puts those of us floundering on the sidelines of the religion to shame. Miqdad remained loyal to Imam Ali (as) and to the religion of Islam both on and off the battlefield.

The Holy Prophet (pbuh) would occasionally send individuals to lead an expedition. These expeditions did not necessarily entail a battle, but soldiers were commanded to be vigilant against any Meccan encroachments. On one occasion he sent Miqdad on an expedition and they met Abu Sufyan's soldiers in an area called Nukhaylah. Miqdad successfully captured three of the opposition including a man by the name of Hakam ibn Kaysan.

Immediately, Umar ibn Khattab, called for Hakam to be beheaded because of his loyalty to Abu Sufyan. Miqdad stopped him and with more cautiousness described how Hakam ibn Kaysan was a nobleman of Mecca who did not have a bad reputation, and in fact he remembered him as a man of good virtues who may have been misled about the Prophet (pbuh).

When Miqdad questioned Hakam it became clear that he had been given false propaganda about Muslims. Miqdad promptly explained to him the reality of the Prophet (pbuh) and his message of monotheism, piety, virtue and justice. Hakam ibn Kaysan became one of the greatest Muslims after this encounter. Hakam is a prominent example of the ability of the human to transform and become a noble representative of truth and justice.

Throughout history even up until today, one sees the same campaign of misinformation and deception about the character of the Holy Prophet (pbuh) and therefore one cannot condemn others who have been misled by these erroneous sources. Instead, every Muslim should be prepared to follow Miqdad in transforming misconceptions about the Holy Prophet (pbuh) and the religion, and foster dialogue and mutual understanding.

In the final years of the life of the Holy Prophet (pbuh), there was a year called 'Aam al-Wufud, the Year of the Delegations. After the conquest of Mecca, in the year 9 AH (after Hijrah), numerous delegations of non-Muslims came to Mecca to meet the Holy Prophet (pbuh) and to learn about Islam. Miqdad observed his father enter amongst a delegation and sought him out to ask him of his intent.

His father related to him that he heard Muhammad (pbuh) took part in wars, and he enjoyed war. Miqdad explained to his father that any warfare on the part of the Muslims was strictly in self-defence, and unlike his father's tribe who relished being aggressors seeking to dominate others, the religion of Islam and Muhammad's (pbuh) goal was to establish a just society that honoured the life, property, honour, intellect, and religion of the human being while recognizing the one true God.

He continued to explain the religion of Islam to his father and slowly brought him towards it. Eventually his father embraced Islam.

Not only had Miqdad become an unswerving and loyal supporter of the Holy Prophet (pbuh) and a devout Muslim, but the narrations state that he remained loyal to Imam Ali (as) and the Ahl al-Bayt (as) as well. This point is a distinguishing factor in the discussions concerning the Companions.

There are many Companions who were good with the Holy Prophet (pbuh) during his lifetime, but after the Holy Prophet (pbuh) died, some of their behaviour left a lot to be desired. This was not the case with Miqdad. For example, there is the story of the food which came from heaven. One day Imam Ali (as) asked Fatimah al-Zahra (as) if there was something for them to eat and she remained silent. He looked at her and he noticed that her face was pale and inquired about the reason.

To this question she replied that there was no food in the house, but that her father had requested her not to trouble Ali ibn Abi Talib (as), so she hadn't complained to him. He comforted her by telling her not to worry, it was not a trouble and he went out to borrow a *dinar* to buy them some food. On his way, he encountered Miqdad and greeted him with the greetings of peace, to which Miqdad returned the greeting of peace but then walked off. It was unusual for Miqdad not to continue the conversation, so he called him back to ask what was the matter.

Miqdad replied that his children had been deprived of food to such a level that their eyes were sunken in the sockets, but he was ashamed to ask Imam Ali (as) for help. Imam Ali (as) gave the one *dinar* he had borrowed for his own family and told Miqdad to feed his children with it.

Then the Imam (as) carried on to the mosque to pray *salat al-maghrib*, the evening prayer, with his father-in-law, the Holy Prophet (pbuh). When his father-in-law (pbuh) finished the prayer, he turned around and requested someone to bring Ali ibn Abi Talib (as) to him. When he did so, he asked Imam Ali (as) if he could come to dinner at his house. Of course the Imam welcomed him generously even though he had nothing to offer him. When they entered the house, Imam Ali (as) informed Fatimah (as) that they had a guest, her blessed father, but she noticed he came home without any food from his outing. Fatimah al-Zahra (as) told him not to worry and went to the kitchen where she recited a verse from the Holy Qur'an.

She supplicated to her Lord:

> Behold! the disciples, said: "O Jesus the son of Mary! can thy Lord send down to us a table spread out (with viands) from heaven?" Said Jesus: "Fear Allah, if ye have faith. (Q5:112) Oh Allah (swt), if for Jesus (pbuh) son of Mary (as), you are willing to bring him food from heaven, I am Fatimah (as), daughter of the Holy Prophet (pbuh). Would you not provide us with food, so that we are able to feed my father?

The narrations state that Jibreel descended with food in response to Fatimah al-Zahra's (as) supplication, and thus they were able to eat and be nourished. Miqdad witnessed this miraculous event confirming for him yet again the divine and spiritual truth of Muhammad and his blessed family.

The Holy Prophet (pbuh) used to say, when I said the verse, "...No reward do I ask of you for this except the love of those near of kin..." (Q42:23) there were six people who unconditionally looked after this command, and Miqdad was part of this spiritually elevated group.

He unreservedly showed love for Aal Muhammad (as) in every action in his life and stood by them at the most critical and important times, such as at the Battle of Badr and Uhud, and later at the event of the Saqifah when Imam Ali ibn Abi Talib's (as) leadership was taken away from him.

Miqdad was one of the five who remained loyal. When Saqifah occurred, six of the Muhajirun and six of the Ansar came to Imam Ali (as) and confirmed their loyalty and his right to leadership. The following day, a few hundred joined Imam Ali (as) and claimed the same.

On the third day, Imam Ali (as) commanded all of those who had claimed loyalty to shave their heads, so he could know if he truly had enough support to obtain his rights. But of the few hundred, only five turned up to Ali (as) and Fatimah (as)'s house with their head shaven.

The five were: Abu Dhar, Salman, Ammar, Miqdad, and some narrations state Zubayr while others say Hudhayfah al-Yamani. They had come to the house confirming their loyalty and willingness to sacrifice their lives. It is on that day that Imam Ali (as) mentioned the famous line, "If only I had forty (soldiers with me), I would have taken my leadership back, but all I had was five, and no more."

Miqdad was also one of the chosen and trusted few who carried the body of Fatimah al-Zahra (as) to her burial. Before her death she had specified that she only would allow certain individuals to attend her burial and funeral prayer. The narrations state that she said, "I only want Miqdad there, Salman, Ammar, and Abu Dhar."

One narration mentions Jabir ibn Abdullah Ansari and Hudhayfah al-Yamani. And from amongst the women, she specified only Fidha, Umm Ayman, and Asma bint Umays. She emphatically did not want anyone else from amongst the inhabitants of Medina to be present at her burial.

Miqdad told Imam Ali (as) under no circumstances would he ever leave him. This pledge was evidenced years after Saqifah when the *shura* (consultation to elect the caliph) occurred some twelve years later, Miqdad was still loyal. Umar ibn Khattab appointed a *shura* of six people to choose the caliph or ruler after him. He said Ali,

Uthman, Abdul Rahman ibn Awf, Saad ibn Abi Waqqas, Talhah and Zubayr would be the ones to choose the next leader.

When Miqdad found out about this plan, he came out in front of everyone and he said, "Listen to me, If Ali ibn Abi Talib (as) is chosen tomorrow, I will obey. If anyone else is chosen, I will disobey his orders..." Miqdad didn't stop there in his courageous support of the rightful leader, but went to one of the six and said, "There was a day when Ali ibn Abi Talib (as) was the only one. Now he is considered one of six."

Miqdad would speak out vigorously for the rights of Imam Ali (as) constantly throughout his life. On one occasion, he reminded the Muslim community, "In spite of all of his sacrifice for the religion of Islam, you refuse to elect him as your caliph and neglect him in your affairs." Sadly, Miqdad's loyalty to the Holy Prophet (pbuh) and his family did not penetrate the heart of his own son. His son, by the name of Abdullah, fought Imam Ali (as) in the Battle of Jamal after the death of Miqdad.

The Imam (as) himself looked at him and addressed him, "Your father, how loyal he was to our cause; he was one of those who used to memorize the Qur'an, he used to teach the Qur'an, and now you come and you fight us?" This turn of events was a great source of sadness; this legacy of love and devotion, this loyalty to Allah and his Holy Prophet (pbuh) did not carry on through his son.

Nevertheless, Miqdad unconditionally showed love for Aal Muhammad (as) in every action throughout his long life. His greatest action, without a doubt, was in the Battle of Badr, a battle that was a deep source of pride for Muslims in their early history. From that battle, his loyalty to the Holy Prophet (pbuh) reverberated throughout the subsequent years and remained in the consciousness of the growing Muslim community.

In fact, an Umayyad caliph who ruled from 717 to 720 CE by the name of Umar ibn Abdul Aziz stopped the cursing of Ali ibn Abi Talib (as) because of the Battle of Badr. Furthermore, he gave the estate of Fadak that had been bequeathed to the daughter of the Prophet (pbuh), but then confiscated, back to the family of the Prophet (pbuh), specifically to the fifth Imam, Imam Muhammad al-Baqir (as). The narrations state that Umar ibn Abdul Aziz would express anger as a young boy at the age of six, he would curse Imam Ali (as). One day his teacher looked at him and frowned. Umar, the six year old, reprimanded his elder teacher for frowning at a prince. His teacher went on to remind him of the great Battle of Badr and the noble warriors who fought in it. Umar replied that he considered them to be great men. The teacher continued by asking the young Umar what he would think about the one warrior who killed half of the opposition single-handedly, and the boy said, "He would be the greatest hero of them all."

That's when the teacher revealed to him that the one you cursed was that great man, Ali ibn Abi Talib (as); this revelation changed Umar and he ruled with more justice, piety, and fairness than his predecessors.

Works Cited

Ibn Abi Talib, Ali. Ed. Mohammad Askari Jafery. *Nahjul Balagha, Peak of Eloquence: Sermons, Letters, and Sayings of Imam Ali Ibn Abu Talib* (Elmhurst, NY: Tahrike Tarsile Quran, 1986).

Shariati, Ali. *Fatima is Fatima*. Trans. Laleh Bakhtiar. (Tehran: The Shariati Foundation, 1982).

Chapter 10:
Ali ibn Abi Talib

I mam Ali ibn Abi Talib (as) was born on the 13th of Rajab in the year 600 and died on the 21st of Ramadan in 40AH/660 CE. He occupies a prominent position within the religion of Islam and is revered as one of the greatest leaders in Islamic history. He was the embodiment of knowledge, generosity, valor, bravery and dedication towards the religion of Islam.

His Parents and Childhood

The Imam's parents, Abu Talib and Fatima bint Asad, were both followers of the monotheistic way of Abraham. A group of believers who lived in Mecca in the early days were followers of the message of Prophet Ibrahim (as) and all the messengers who came after Ibrahim (as). They are classified under the term "Hanifs." When Abu Talib read the marriage ceremony of the Prophet (pbuh) to Lady Khadija, he mentioned very clearly within his sermon that, "I am the follower of one God and the follower of the Prophets of God, especially the Prophets who descended from the line of Prophet Ibrahim (as)." Therefore Abu Talib and Fatima bint Asad were both Abrahamic monotheists in terms of their belief.

Their faith is also seen in the words of Fatima bint Asad during the time when she used to circumambulate the Ka'ba. There were two types of people who circumambulated the Ka'ba at that time.

There were those who believed in one God but started making images for that God in the form of idols; and then there was a group who believed in one God and would not associate any images with that God. When Fatima bint Asad used to circumambulate the Ka'ba, she would recite a supplication that is still with us until today. She said, "O Allah! In the name of Your Majesty, and in the name of Your Power, and in the name of the Prophets You sent from the line of Ibrahim (as), help me in this period with the pangs of labor and the pangs of childbirth and make it easy for me."

The narrations are clear, both in the books of the Imamis and in other schools in Islam. For example, if one studies the works of Imam Hakim an-Nisaburi in his book *al-Mustadrak ala'l-Sahihayn*, or Mas'udi in his book, *Muruj al-Dhahab*, all of them state that when Fatima bint Asad said these words near the Casaba, the Casaba opened up for her and she entered it. She stayed within it for three days, an honor that Islamic history has only reserved for Imam Ali b. Abi Talib (as).

You will find that there are some other historical references to other people being born in the Ka'ba but this was a group of people who tried to diminish the significance of Imam Ali b. Abi Talib (as). The fact remains that the only man to receive the honor of being born in the Casaba is Imam Ali (as). When his mother emerged from the Casaba on the fourth day, the first person to welcome her was the Prophet (pbuh). He welcomed her and took Ali from her hands, and from that day, the Prophet (pbuh) embraced Ali throughout his childhood; he would chew food before he placed it in the mouth of Ali; and Imam Ali himself narrates that, "I would follow the Prophet in those early days like a child of the she-camel would follow its mother...I used to see the light of revelation and I would hear the words of Prophethood...When the religion consisted of only three people, it was always me and Khadija alongside the Prophet."

In other words, from an early age Abu Talib turned his sons and his children towards the religion of Islam; Imam Ali b. Abi Talib (as) had three elder brothers. His oldest brother was Talib, hence their father's name was Abu Talib. Talib died at the age of fifty-five; the second eldest brother was 'Aqil. He died at the age of ninety-three; then the third eldest was Ja'far who died at the age of forty; and finally the Imam. The Prophet (pbuh) was thirty when the Imam was born. Imam Ali also had two sisters - one was named Fakhita (Um Hani) and the other was named Jumana. Thus, Abu Talib and Fatima bint Asad had six children.

Due to the extreme difficulty many Arabs were facing at the time, the Prophet (pbuh) came to Abu Talib and said, "Let my uncles Hamza and Abbas and I take responsibility for your children." Abu Talib asked, "Whom would you like to care for?" He said, "Let me bring up Ali."

Thus the Prophet (pbuh) wanted to bring up the young Imam in the way that Abu Talib had brought him up. It was only ten years later when Imam Ali was ten that Prophet Muhammad (pbuh) announced his prophethood. In those early days there were only a few reverts, like Ammar b. Yasir, Bilal and Abu Dharr al-Ghiffari.

A Momentous Incident in the Life of the Imam

From a young age Imam Ali b. Abi Talib (as) had the maturity to assist in carrying the message of the religion.

That is why when Da'wat Dhul 'Ashira occurred after Allah revealed the verse, "Invite and warn your nearest relatives," (Q26:214), the Prophet (pbuh) told the young Ali, "I want you to do something for me."

"What is it, O Prophet?"

"I want you to prepare a meal for me."

"Which meal?" asked Ali.

"Get a sheep, one kilo of wheat and three kilos of yogurt. I want you to make a feast and I want you to invite our uncles." The Prophet (pbuh) and Imam Ali were cousins, so they both had the same set of uncles. When they came that day, a momentous incident occurred in the life of Imam Ali b. Abi Talib (as).

When they arrived at his house, the Prophet (pbuh) said to them, "Welcome to my house. I have glad tidings to give you about the message." Abu Lahab did not listen to him. But the second time they came, the Prophet (pbuh) said to them, "You know that I am truthful and you know that I am trustworthy and you know that I have not lied to any of you. I have come to bring you a message of goodness, to worship only one God and not associate partners with Him, and that there is a Day of Judgment where you will be accountable for all your acts, and that there is no difference between the male and female, or between black and white." Abu Lahab looked at him and said, "O Muhammad, what is this sorcery that you are trying to bewitch us with?" The Prophet (pbuh) said, "Whoever amongst you accepts me as his Prophet will be my caliph and successor after me."

From a young age Ali was already instructed with that message that he was to be the successor of the Prophet (pbuh) because Ali, at the age of thirteen, raised his hands and said, "O Prophet of God, I will listen to your message and I am the first to accept your words."

Abu Lahab turned around to Abu Talib and said, "Abu Talib, it looks like one day your son will have to lead you!" He tried to mock him. In the books of our Sunni brothers it says that Abu Talib came to Ali and said to him, "Ali, are you sure you want to accept this message? Are you ready for it?"

Ali, full of maturity at that young age, replied by saying, "O my father, Allah did not ask me when He created me, therefore I do not need to ask anyone when I surrender to Him (swt)."

Thus it is written in Sunni sources as well that Ali (as) had the maturity to understand the message of our Prophet (pbuh) at that young age. Not only did he have the maturity, but he gained the honour of becoming the successor of the Prophet (pbuh).

Thus, from that young age, the Prophet (pbuh) would constantly give him duties in order to allow him to mature and develop in the religion. At the age of twenty-four, when the whole of Mecca had decided to combat the message of the Prophet (pbuh), the Prophet (pbuh) came to Ali (as) and said, "Ali, they have decided to kill me; a number of them are going to come together and kill me, so would you do a task for me?"

Ali said, "O Prophet of God, what is the task?"

The Prophet (pbuh) said, "I want you to sleep in my bed. Are you ready to sacrifice your soul for the message of the religion of Islam?"

He said, "O Prophet, will you be safe?"

The Prophet (pbuh) said, "Yes, I will."

He said, "Then my soul is dedicated to your soul and my spirit is dedicated to your spirit." Then he went into prostration and said three times, "Shukran lillah! Shukran lillah! Shukran lillah! All thanks is to Allah!"

That night when the enemies came to attack, they saw Ali sleeping in the bed of the Prophet (pbuh). After that the Prophet (pbuh) said to him, "Ali, I want you to perform a task. There are a number of my enemies who have deposited their trusts with me. I find no one better in this religion but you to return the trusts back to them."

Hanzala, the son of Abu Sufyan, heard that Ali had remained behind and was returning everyone trusts. Hanzala, the oldest son of Abu Sufyan, wanted to create some trouble. He told Umayr b. Wa'il, who was a poor man, to do something for him. He bribed him with 350 grams of gold and a particular necklace which Umayr's wife used to admire when she would see it on Hind's neck. Hind was Hanzala's mother. Umayr's wife had always wanted to wear that necklace even if it was only for a day. It was a very precious necklace that was made with 35 grams of gold. Thus, Hanzala promised Umayr that if he did the job for him he could keep that necklace for life.

Umayr b. Wa'il was related to the tribe of Banu Thaqif (the tribe of Hajjaj b. Yusuf and Mukhtar al-Thaqafi). He told Umayr, "I want you to go to Ali, the representative of Muhammad, who is near the Casaba right now, and tell him that you entrusted 250 grams gold with the Prophet (pbuh) and that you want it back." Hanzala wanted to defame the Prophet (pbuh), who was beginning to win the hearts of the people as they received their trusts. If Imam Ali (as) said that he did not have Umayr's trust, they could claim that the Prophet (pbuh) had returned all the small items but took away the more valuable ones. This would help to create some doubt in the people's minds about the Prophet (pbuh). Furthermore, if Imam Ali did not deny their claim, he might give them the money in order to save the Prophet (pbuh)'s reputation.

Thus Umayr agreed to the plan but said, "Ali will not believe me. He will first ask me for a witness." Hanzala said, "I will provide the witnesses. Write the name of these witnesses down: Abu Jahal, Akrama b. Abu Jahal, Utbah, Abu Sufyan and myself. Now you have the name of all five witnesses." Umayr was now satisfied and went to Imam Ali (as), who, by now, had returned all the belongings of the people. He was about to leave when Umayr approached him and said, "O son of Abu Talib! Where are you going?" Imam said, "I had a responsibility to do which I have done, and now I am going home." Umayr said, "But I have come to obtain my trust. I had left 80 mithqal (grams) of gold and a special trust in a bag. Please give it back to me." Obviously, Imam Ali knew something was suspicious, so he smiled and said, "Really? You gave 80 mithqal of gold and a special trust?" Umayr said, "Yes."

Everyone was still present there as they were opening their bags and checking their items. Imam Ali addressed them and said, "This brother of mine has come to claim his trust. Please remain seated so I can solve this problem." Then Imam addressed Umayr and said, "Okay, tell me who are your witnesses?" Umayr took the five names Hanzala had given him. Now Imam Ali asked Umayr in front of everyone, "Okay, tell me, when did you give this trust to my Prophet?" Umayr said, "It was at sunrise." Imam asked, "So when the Prophet took the trust, what did he do with it?" Umayr said, "As he was leaving for the haram, he took the trust and put it in his pocket."

Imam Ali said, "Okay, now call your first witness. Who is it?" He said, "Akrama b. Abu Jahal."

Some youths went and called Akrama and he came to the scene. By this time everyone present became very interested in the whole case. When Akrama came, Umayr was told to sit quietly without uttering a word. Now Imam asked Akrama, "Umayr has stated that he had given an trust to my Prophet, are you a witness to that?"

Akrama said, "Yes I am."

Imam said, "Okay, so tell me, what time was this trust given?" Now Akrama was in a predicament. After some thinking, he said, "It was early in the morning."

Imam said, "Okay, then what did my Prophet do with it?"

He said, "Well, because he was returning from the haram, he took it and went to his house." Imam said, "Okay, now sit down." He looked at Umayr and said, "Who is your second witness?" Umayr said, "Abu Jahal."

Now Abu Jahal was called to the scene. Imam said, "O Hisham, Umayr is saying that you are a witness to the trusts that he gave the Prophet.

Tell me, what time was it when the trust was given?" Abu Jahal said, "I do not know anything. Do not involve me in this! I am not a witness to anything." Imam looked at Umayr and said, "Who is your third witness?" He said, "Utbah."

Utbah was a senior leader of the Quraysh. He was called and asked the same thing. He said, "It was afternoon and the Prophet was going towards Khadija's house and so he told his slave to go and put the trust in his aunt's (Fatima bint Asad's) house."

Imam Ali said to Umayr, "Now who is your next witness?"

He said, "Abu Sufyan." Abu Sufyan was called and asked the same question. He said, "It was the time of Asr and the Prophet was sitting in the haram at the time. He took the trust and kept it with him."

Imam Ali asked Umayr, "Now who is your fifth witness?"

He said, "Hanzala b. Abu Sufyan."

Hanzala said, "It was nighttime and the Prophet gave the trust to his slave and sent it to Khadija's house."

By now all the people heard the testimonies and the contradiction between all their statements. The witnesses themselves were getting extremely embarrassed listening to the contradictory statements. Umayr b. Wa'il Thaqafi was so embarrassed during this whole process that he said, "Oh Ali, forgive me. I made a big mistake. These people bribed me and told me to do this." Thus, their plan was foiled.

The Prophet (pbuh) had already gone towards Medina and left Ali (as) with the responsibility of caring for his trusts, which included the safety of the female members of his family. Ali guaranteed their protection as he escorted them to Medina.

Many people fail to acknowledge how unsafe the journey was for Imam Ali b. Abi Talib (as). Many think that only the Prophet and Abu Bakr had an unsafe journey. They do not realize that the enemies of Islam had set their eyes on Ali when the Quraysh could not catch up with the Prophet (pbuh). It was in that journey that they realized that they had a warrior on their hands. The Prophet (pbuh) was waiting for Imam Ali in the city of Quba, as he did not want to enter Medina without him. So when Imam Ali b. Abi Talib (as) reached Medina, his body was bloody and full of injuries. The Quraysh had ambushed him on the way and he fought them on his own and protected the ladies. It was in that journey that he showed his valor and bravery.

Honors Bestowed on Imam Ali (as) During the life of the Prophet

The moment they reached Medina, the Prophet (pbuh) did two things to honor Imam Ali. First, the Prophet (pbuh) made the pact of brotherhood between the Ansar and the Muhajireen. The Prophet (pbuh) did not want any tension between the two groups so he made each Ansar a partner and brother of each Muhajir. For example, Abu Bakr was paired with Kharija b. Zohair al-Khazraji; Umar became a brother to Eital b. Malik; Uthman was made a partner of Aws b. Thabit. The people asked, "O Prophet, who is your brother?" He said, "For me, it is only Ali b. Abi Talib; Ali is to me like Aaron was to Moses, except that there is no Prophet after me."

There were some houses that shared a common wall with the mosque. People had built doors in their houses which opened to the mosque for their convenience. Allah ordered that all doors should be sealed off except for that of the Prophet and Imam Ali. This was another honor given to him by Allah.

His Battles

Imam Ali (as), at the age of twenty-four, in his first battle for Islam at Badr, then Uhud, Khandaq and Khaybar, showed a distinction like no other on the battlefield. In Islamic history, many individuals have been described as great warriors but there is not a single warrior in Islamic history that came near the dust of Ali b. Abi Talib (as). He had an unrivaled distinction in the battlefield. At Badr, he destroyed half of the opposition alone. At Uhud, the Prophet was alone on the mountain; Ali, Miqdad, Ammar, Abu Dujana Ansari and a lady called al-Harithiyya were the ones who helped him. It was on that day that the famous cry could be heard, "There is no youth but Ali and no sword but Dhulfikar!"

At Khandaq and Khaybar, he displayed a spiritual side to him, which showed that he had a balance of opposite qualities, and thus, he was a complete human being. Warriors are normally reckless; and not only are they reckless but they tend to be arrogant as well. These two combinations usually are an integral part of a warrior's personality; they are either reckless or arrogant. One hardly finds any ethics in warriors and it is very rare to find any spirituality in them.

However, Imam Ali b. Abi Talib (as) remarkably displayed piety, humility and courage all at once.

Imam Ali's humility and piety in his duel with Amr b. Abd al-Wud was already mentioned above (in chapter one). At the Battle of Khaybar, Imam Ali b. Abi Talib (as) lifted a gate which none could lift. Here we are not concerned with what he lifted, but rather with what allows one to be so powerful. After Khaybar he came back from the battle and began to cry. He was asked, "O son of Abu Talib! Why do you cry? You have just lifted the gate others could not lift!"

He replied, "I cannot bear to see the Jewish soldiers with a rope around their hands. Loosen their rope. Are they not human beings?" Then he returned home and his wife Fatima (as) offered him some bread. He was known for his piety, and that he would only eat dry bread, because he would say, "How can I eat soft bread when there are poor people in the Muslim world?" He tried to break the bread, but the bread did not break. They said, "O son of Abu Talib! You lifted a gate which forty men together could not lift, and you cannot break a piece of bread?"

He said, "The gate I lifted for Allah; the bread I am trying to break is for Ali. I lifted the gate of Khaybar, not with my physical strength, but with the strength of my Ruh! If I can understand my soul, then I can understand my Lord; and the moment I can understand my Lord, everything is easy before me."

In the Battle of Hunayn as well, were it not for Ali remaining behind, this religion would have been destroyed. The greatest performance of Imam Ali b. Abi Talib (as) was at Hunayn, and not necessarily at Badr, Uhud, Khaybar or Khandaq. Imam Zayn ul-Abideen (as) said in Syria, "I am the son of the one who fought at Badr and Hunayn!" Imam Ali b. Abi Talib (as), at Hunayn, was left alone against the opposition and finished them off.

After the Death of the Prophet (pbuh)

The Prophet (pbuh) was sixty-three years old when he died. Imam Ali b. Abi Talib (as) was thirty-three years old at the time. The Prophet (pbuh) had told the people, "This is my successor; be loyal to him; do not deceive him or be cunning to him or attack him; he is not just my son-in-law, he is appointed by Allah to look after my message," but the people ended up taking away the leadership of Imam Ali b. Abi Talib (as). They took his leadership, and they attacked his wife and killed her, and he was left with four orphans in his house. Yet did Imam Ali b. Abi Talib (as) allow his ego to get to him? Imam Ali b. Abi Talib (as) said, "The religion of Islam is more important than causing disunity. I will remain silent, but when I see injustice, I will speak out against it."

When the Prophet (pbuh) died, Imam Ali b. Abi Talib (as) was thirty-three, and he became the fourth caliph at the age of fifty-eight. Some people ask, did Ali b. Abi Talib do anything for Islam in those twenty-five years? Even though Imam Ali b. Abi Talib (as) was not the caliph chosen at Saqifa, he was still the caliph for Ammar, Bilal, Salman, Abu Dharr and so on. Therefore, when Imam Ali b. Abi Talib (as) saw any injustice during that time, he would speak out and he would not just remain silent. He taught us an ethical lesson: when you see injustice or tyranny of any type, be it big or small, never remain silent against it.

One day a lady came to Umar b. Khattab, the second caliph, and said, "I have committed adultery." Umar asked, "Were there witnesses?" She said, "Yes, there were witnesses and I am willing to be punished."

Umar said, "Very well," and told his men to punish her. She said, "But do you mind if Ali b. Abi Talib makes the decision?"

Umar said, "Why?"

She said, "Because I believe that Ali b. Abi Talib is the most just human living on this earth. I know that he was brought up in the lap of the Prophet. So who else can teach justice but Muhammad?"

Umar called Imam Ali b. Abi Talib (as) and told him to pass the judgment on her. When Imam Ali b. Abi Talib (as) came, he asked her, "What is your crime?"

She said, "I committed adultery."

Imam said, "What were the circumstances?"

She said, "I had no food for my children and I went to ask for help from one of the rich men of the area. He said to me, 'If you want food, you have to commit adultery with me.' I told him, 'O man, fear God. Do not say such words.' I pleaded the second time but the third time I gave in."

Imam Ali said to her, "Very well, you are free to leave."

She said, "What do you mean?"

He said, "Chapter 5, verse 3."

She said, "What do you mean?" She looked at Umar inquiringly and said, "What does he mean?"

Umar too asked the Imam, "What do you mean?"

Imam said, "Chapter 5, verse 3 says, 'Those who are compelled to sin while they are in a state of hunger, Allah forgives their sin.'" This lady was compelled to sin, but she was in a state of hunger. Allah forgives those in a state of hunger because the shame is on the state not on the people. The state should not allow a lady to be in such a situation.) It was at times like these that Umar was heard saying, "If it were not for Ali, Umar would have perished!"

Thus Imam Ali always came to help when he was summoned. There was an instance when Umar was going to fight the Romans. The army was leaving and Imam Ali stopped him from going even though he was all dressed to leave. Imam Ali said, "You are the caliph of the time if you go forward and your army gets killed they will know you have no more reinforcements as you will already be there. Stay behind. It is better for you." This guidance was to save Islam. It was the role of these representatives to ensure that Islam did not lose its position in its infancy.

When Uthman, the third caliph, appointed his family members, the Umayyads, to different positions of authority, Imam Ali would speak out and would not remain silent.

His Knowledge

In those twenty-five years when he was not the caliph he would publicly proclaim, "Ask me! Ask me whatever you wish before you do not find me! I know the ways of the heavens much more than I do the ways of the earth!" It was a challenge. The non-Muslims would come to Medina and ask, "Where is Ali b. Abi Talib?" The people would say, "Why?" They would say, "We hear that he is the successor to the Prophet; we want to ask him questions that none can answer. If he can answer them, then we will follow him."

One Jewish man came to Imam Ali b. Abi Talib (as) and said to him, "You claim to be the successor of Muhammad?"

The Imam said, "Yes."

The visitor said, "I am going to ask you a mathematical question which no human can answer and it is written in the religious scriptures; and only the successor of Muhammad can answer this."

"Go ahead."

"Which number, if you divide it by any number between one and ten, remains a whole number?"

"Two thousand five hundred and twenty."

"Sorry?" "Two thousand five hundred and twenty." "How did you get that?"

"The number of days in the week multiplied by the number of days in the year." The man looked puzzled and said, "Okay, in the Arabian calendar there are three hundred and sixty days in the year and there are seven days in the week."

Imam said, "So multiply three hundred and sixty by seven. What do you get?"

He said, "2520."

Imam said, "Divide 2520 by 1. What do you get?"

He said, "2520."

Imam said, "By two?"

He said, "1260."

Imam said, "By three?"

He said, "840."

"By four?"

"630."

"By five?"

"504."

"By six?"

"420."

"By seven?"

"360."

"By eight?"

"315."

"By nine?"

"280."

"By ten?"

"252." The Jew said, "Truly, this is Ali b. Abi Talib." (2520 divided by any number between one and ten is the only number in the world that comes out whole.)

Thus people would keep approaching him to ask for knowledge until he became the caliph.

His Life as a Caliph

The tragedy in this religion is that the Muslims did not utilise Imam Ali b. Abi Talib (as) like they could have. During his four years as a caliph, there were three civil wars fought against him. In each of those wars the dignity that he displayed in them is a message for each Muslim today; that even when another Muslim acts rudely towards you, if you are a follower of Ali b. Abi Talib, act tolerantly towards them. There may be Muslims today who look towards the Imamis and are disrespectful towards them, who may call them the people of innovation, who may call them the people of shirk. One must not reply by falling to their level; one must maintain one's dignity like the Imam maintained his dignity.

At Jamal, he saw that the lady fighting him was the wife of the Prophet; others around him said, "Show disrespect."

He said, "Never!" Ali treated the wife of the Prophet (pbuh) with the same dignity she received before the war. When he sent her back to Medina with respect she turned around and said to him, "You are the killer of the beloved ones!"

He replied, "If I am the killer of the beloved ones, then I would have killed people like Marwan and Abdullah b. Zubayr (upon victory), but I do not want disunity in the Muslim Ummah." Thus the School of Ahlulbayt (as) should never open the door for disunity.

In Siffin, Mu'awiya's army was able to take control of the water. Imam told his soldiers, "Ask Mu'awiya to allow us to drink water. We are thirsty." Mu'awiya said, "I will never give them any water." Imam told the soldiers to go and win the water back. The soldiers won the water back and the water was then in the possession of Imam Ali (as). Then, Imam Ali's army was informed that the soldiers of Mu'awiya were thirsty. They came to the soldiers of Ali and said, "Please give us water." Imam looked at his soldiers and said, "Do you think we should give them water?" The soldiers said, "No, do not give it to them; they do not deserve it as they did not give us water." Imam said, "No. I cannot bear to see a horse thirsty, let alone a human being."

In the Battle of Nahrawan, the Khawarij, who had once been soldiers in his army, came to fight him. He was in one-on-one combat with one of them. During the combat, the Dhulfikar captured the sword of the opponent and Imam had two swords now. That soldier looked at the Imam and said, "What are you going to do? Are you going to finish me?"

Imam said, "What would you like?"

He said, "I hear Ali b. Abi Talib never rejects a request from a person."

Imam said, "Ask me."

He said, "I want the swords."

Imam said, "Take them."

The man said, "I want to join your path."

Imam said, "No. Say, 'I want to join the path of Allah for justice'; do not look at me. Every drop of my existence is for Allah (swt)!" That is why adopting the sublime character of Ali b. Abi Talib is what makes one a loyal follower.

After the Battle of Nahrawan, he was walking from the battlefield and saw a lady. He came near her and saw her boiling some water and stirring it. He said to her, "O lady, what's wrong? I see you stirring some water." She said, "May God curse the son of Abu Talib!" He said, "Why do you say this?" She said, "At Nahrawan he killed my brothers, my sons and my husband. He came back alive and they came back dead. May God curse him. If I were to meet him one day, I would tell him how much I hate him."

He said, "How are you now?"

She said, "Look at me. I have orphan children and no one to help." After that day, every morning Imam would carry the wheat and make her bread. One day this lady's daughter returned home to see her mother. When she entered the house, she saw the Imam leaving. They exchanged greetings and the Imam left. She recognized the Imam and was mesmerized. She turned around and told her mother, "Mother, did you see who walked in?" The mother said, "I do not know. He is a very generous and humble man but I do not know his name."

She said, "That was Ali b. Abi Talib."

The mother said, "That's Ali?"

She said, "Yes."

The mother said, "I have been cursing him every morning to his face!"

She ran back to the Imam and said, "O son of Abu Talib! Forgive me! I did not know your true character."

Imam said, "O lady, forgive me if I ever hurt you in the name of Allah (swt)." We must assess our actions and question our identity as followers of Ali if our deeds do not resemble his behaviour.

During his caliphate nobody loved him as much as the non-Muslims of his time. The Muslims were the ones fighting him whereas the Christians and Jews loved him and mourned him. Imam Ali has a famous line in his letter to Malik al-Ashtar, which Kofi Annan of the United Nations declared, "The greatest letter of a government ever written by a human being." Imam Ali told Malik in that letter, "Know that people are of two types; they are either your brother in faith or your equal in humanity."

In another line, which should be cemented on the walls of our mosques, Imam said, "Know O Muslims! Our enemy is not the Christians nor the Jews; our enemy is our own ignorance!"

When he walked passed a church, his companion said to him, "I wonder how much polytheism is being done by the people in the church?" Imam said, "I wonder how much monotheism is being practiced." One looked at the cup as half empty; Ali would look at the cup as half full.

When he would walk in the streets, he would see an old Christian begging. Imam would ask, "Why is this Christian begging? When he was young he would work and look after us and now he is old, no one looks after him? I will not move from my position until one of you promises to sponsor this Christian."

There was a Jewish man who cried when he heard that Ali (as) had died. They asked him why he was crying. He said, "I was walking towards Kufa to my home. I met a man and we started talking and I told him I'm Jewish and he said he was Muslim. We kept on talking and walking. I remembered that at the beginning of the conversation he had said that he was going to Kufa; but now as we were walking, we went past Kufa and were going towards my house. So I turned around to him and said, 'O man, you said you are going towards Kufa; why are you still walking with me?' The man said, 'Because in Islam we are taught that the right of the person who travels with us is that we do not leave them until they give us permission. You never gave me permission, so I kept on walking to your house.'

I said, 'Go ahead. I give you permission. Today I have learnt about your religion through your morals.'"

The narrations state that as soon as Ali left, another friend approached the Jewish man and said, "How did you form a relationship with him?" The Jew said, "What do you mean?"

He said, "Do you know who that was?"

The Jew said, "No. He was just one of the Muslims who lives in part of the empire."

He said, "That is the head of the empire!"

The Jew said, "He was Ali b. Abi Talib?"

He said, "Yes."

The Jew said, "The caliph of the whole Muslim empire?"

He said, "Yes, but why did he come to this Jewish area?"

The Jew said, "Would you believe, he said that the rights in Islam of a traveller is that you have to wait for their permission before they let you go."

These were the morals of Imam Ali b. Abi Talib (as) until the day he died. After ibn Muljim struck him, one may ask, which human being says, "Give water to my killer, he is thirsty?" Which human being says, "Feed my killer what you are going to feed me?" Which human being says, "Give shelter to my killer in the way you have given shelter to me?"

Rajiv Gandhi said, "I would never enter a cabinet meeting in my government without giving a new minister Ali's letter to Malik al-Ashtar."

The famous American philosopher, Ralph Emerson, said, "No human can understand the essence of humanity like Ali b. Abi Talib…A human being; in one minute he is a warrior, the next minute he is a leader; the next minute he is a man of knowledge and the next minute he is a man of philosophy. Have you seen a human being this rounded?" Look at his words. Which human says, 'O mankind! You came as a drop of semen and you leave as a piece of dust; you do not now when you came and you do not know when you are going, so why do you walk around like you know everything?' Which human would say, 'Mankind know yourself, then you will know your Lord.' Which human would look at the peacock and say, 'The peacock is the clearest sign of an arrogant creation that is insecure because the peacock makes you look at its feathers because it is insecure about its skinny legs.' Which human being has understood the essence of worship [so well] that he says, 'God, I do not worship you because of my fear of hell because that's the worship of a slave; and I do not worship you because of my love of heaven because that's the worship of a businessman; I worship you because you are worthy of worship. That's the worship of a free man."

Read the supplications of Kumayl and Mashlul which are spoken from the tongue of Imam Ali b. Abi Talib (as). A befitting line from a Sikh poet, Kinor Singh, reads, "O Ali! You belong to every faith, every age and all people. We will never let anyone take your honour and we will never let anyone claim you as their own because Ali b. Abi Talib belongs to every human being!"

ABOUT THE AUTHOR

Dr. Sayed Ammar Nakshawani is regarded as one of the most powerful speakers in the Muslim world. He was born in 1981 and graduated from the University College, London, as well as the London School of Economics. He was then awarded with an MA in Islamic Studies from Shahid Beheshti University in Iran.

Dr. Nakshawani completed his PhD thesis at the University of Exeter. He has lectured at the university in Classical Islamic History and then pursued further studies at the Islamic Seminary in Damascus, Syria. Currently he is a visiting scholar at the Centre of Islamic Studies, University of Cambridge.

He has written three other English language books - Ramadan Sermons, The Fourteen Infallibles and Hujr b Adi: A Victim of Terror. His fourth book, in the French language, was released in August 2013 with a Foreword by Prof Tariq Ramadan on Islam and France today.

For more detailed information and past lectures logon
to www.sayedammar.com

Made in the USA
Lexington, KY
11 June 2014